KING OF CLUBS

KING

OF

CLUBS

❧

Robert H. Dedman

with Debbie DeLoach

TAYLOR PUBLISHING COMPANY,
DALLAS, TEXAS

Published by Taylor Publishing Company
1550 West Mockingbird Lane
Dallas, Texas 75235

Special thanks to Patricia Baldwin, Editor-in-Chief of Private Clubs magazine

Book design by Mark McGarry
Set in Goudy

Library of Congress Cataloging-in-Publication Data
    Dedman, Robert H.
        King of clubs : grow rich in more than money / by Robert H. Dedman, with
Debbie DeLoach.
            p.   cm.
    ISBN 0-87833-202-2
        1. Success. 2. Dedman, Robert H. 3. Businessmen—United States
—Biography. I. DeLoach, Debbie. II. Title.
    bj1611.d365   1998
    158.1—dc21   98-27164
                                                        CIP

Printed in the United States of America
10 9 8 7 6 5 4

To Nancy, my wife, my love, my life, my role model.

Her belief in me has enriched my victories.
Her support of me has helped lessen my defeats.
Her graciousness toward me has compensated for my mistakes.
Her love for me has brightened my life here on Earth beyond
belief.
We are partners in the truest sense of the word...in all that we
have done and all that we have left to do.
With all my love and gratitude.

Contents

Acknowledgment

I've been fortunate through the years to be surrounded by people who spend their lives being nice. Like Brenda McCord. She's been my executive assistant since November 21, 1981. I still can't believe she's been able to put up with me for that long. She is a living, breathing "be nice" machine. Always upbeat. Always positive. Always composed. Always responsible. Always there. It's delightful to know that she's going to do the responsible thing in a very gracious way every day of her life. I absolutely adore who she is and hope I never have to do without her. I recently told one fellow that if he whisked her away to California, I'd shoot him. Of course, I was kidding…almost.

Foreword
By Dr. Robert Schuller

I have a lot in common with Robert Dedman. You could even say we were cut from the same cloth. Humble circumstances brought us both into this world, but we soon learned about helping hands. They were at the end of our own arms. Our lives have been full of hard work and blessed with good fortune. Our timing and tenacity have bestowed upon us more success than anyone could possibly deserve. And to borrow from the poet Robert Browning, we're both at *"the last of life for which the first was made."* The big difference is we now know it takes more than money to be rich in life.

There's something else we have in common...we love to talk. We both use our voices, hopefully, for the good of others. I do most of mine in front of millions of television viewers every Sunday morning. "The Hour of Power" program from the Crystal Cathedral is broadcast around the world. Standing at that pulpit every week is pure soul food for someone who feels he has a message. Using a four-legged chair as his prop, Robert is in high demand for his "P-L-A-N" talk at commencement exercises and professional meetings. He is always eager to motivate others, and has done so all over the world for more than twenty years.

To present this man to an audience poses a real problem, though. I know! He's been on "The Hour of Power" program twice, so I've had the pleasure—and problem—of introducing him myself. How do you introduce a man who has four college degrees, a major college, and a major medical center named after him while he's still alive? A man who has already made millions and is determined to give most of it away by the time he dies. A man who quotes Kipling, Browning, Shakespeare, Emerson, and Longfellow like they were his golf partners. And a man who is living proof that nice guys don't always finish last.

I could tell the audience was impressed, and so was Robert. Upon hearing such a brief, albeit laudatory, introduction, he said that he felt somewhat compelled to commence his brief remarks with a very short prayer. "Heavenly Father, please forgive Dr. Schuller for such an overly generous introduction, and please forgive me for enjoying it so much."

You may or may not know who Robert Dedman is. If you have heard of him, you might be more familiar with ClubCorp, the company he founded in 1957, and his reputation acquired since as the "richest guy in golf." He's made a billion bucks and already given away over $100 million. Even more likely, though, you know more about ClubCorp's people and properties, such as the famous Pinehurst Resort & Country Club in North Carolina where the next U.S. Open is going to be held, and The Homestead resort in Hot Springs, Virginia, the oldest resort in America started in 1766 and home of the oldest first tee in continuous use here.

I met Robert in 1989 when we both were inducted into the Horatio Alger Association. I've since learned that he delights almost everyone he knows with his philosophies about what truly counts in life. A menagerie of lifetime experiences taught him what rich really is. Rich in friends, rich in family, rich in health, rich in values, rich in outlook, rich in spiritual well-being, and rich in money and business. These insights are in the pages that follow, or I'm sure he wouldn't have agreed to write this book. He's the last one to ever write a book to pay tribute to himself. That's not his style.

As a man, there's a poem that summarizes Robert (to a tee, if you'll pardon my pun). Written by William Earnest Henley, "The Invictus," which means "unconquerable" in Latin, the last two lines read, "*I am the master of my fate. I am the captain of my soul.*" I wrote a lot about that in my own book, *If It's Going To Be, It's Up To Me*. Whatever people make of themselves is really up to them. God can help, but He can't do it for us. Anything worth having is worth the blood, sweat, and tears it takes to get there. No matter how bad the circumstances, how humble our beginnings, we can all be winners.

A rich life has nothing to do with money, success, or possessions. It's all about greatness, and greatness is inherent in all of us. True wealth is a matter of spirit, and so is Robert.

Preface

You're now reading a book written by a country boy from a poor family in south central Arkansas. That's where I came from. Those are my roots. Where I am now came from having a good idea at the right time, the know-how, and the good fortune to make it work, a passion for poetry that turned into a philosophy for success, and a belief that it takes more than money to be truly rich in life.

You probably already know that money is not the solution to every problem. In fact, money often creates more problems than it solves. Money can do much good, as well as bad, but it cannot buy a rich life. That quality of life is created, nurtured, and later, hopefully, admired. Balance, humor, giving, living, loving, laughing, learning, time-budgeting, having integrity, being nice, working hard, and playing even harder all equate to a richness beyond dollars and cents. These insights, which have come to be known *around ClubCorp* as "Robert's Rules of Order," are what I wish to share with you in this book.

Writing this book was almost easy, compared with deciding how to organize it. After all, my rules of order are not set in stone. They change from time to time and increase or decrease in number, depending upon the current situation. For the purposes of this book, I stuck with ten. You no doubt will have additions, subtractions, and substitutions, too, if you take the time to examine your own life and decide which principles are important to you. Mine simply represent a good starting position in a race that ultimately everyone would like to win.

Along the way, you'll learn more about the vehicle I used to achieve business success—ClubCorp, which I actually commenced as a moonlighting, night-time, weekend, holiday pursuit. I'll also talk about some of the proven management skills that have contributed to ClubCorp's prosperity. Robert's Rules of Order are the foundation upon which ClubCorp was built. They are inter-related and dependent on each other to create and complete a total picture. Individually, they may seem more like bricks and mortar, but together, they support a composite whole...a culture...a company today called ClubCorp.

I'd also like you to know that this book, about the richness of life, is not about making more money for me. All of my share of royalties from book sales will go to five primary recipients: Southern Methodist University in Dallas, Texas; The University of Texas Exes Foundation in Austin; the Robert Schuller Foundation in Newport Beach, California; The University of North Texas in Denton; and the Florida State University Alumni Club in Tallahassee for books purchased by people associated with those organizations. The balance will go to the Dedman Foundation to continue to aid the causes that my wife Nancy and I have supported during our lifetimes, and hopefully long after our deaths.

I suspect this life is *not* a dress rehearsal. It's probably the real thing. We must enjoy it and get all we can out of it because it may be the only chance we get. Even if there's another one hereafter, it's actually difficult to imagine a merciful God giving someone another life who doesn't enjoy this one. Think about it! If this one isn't full of love, laughter, giving, and living, then why would you even want another one?

There is a sign on my office wall that reads, "It's What You

Learn After You Know It All That Really Counts." I hope that this book is filled with learning about things you may think you know all about. When I was young, I thought I knew it all, too. Now I'm even learning how to admit I was wrong, but my reward has been a greater knowledge about living a rich life that goes far beyond my net worth.

Every life, yours and mine, is a story. Each day we live is full of hope, joy, despair, excitement, disappointment, new beginnings, and ultimate endings. This story just happens to be mine. I've lived an extraordinary life for an ordinary guy, and wrote this book because I thought it might benefit others. May its contents help you be successful in your endeavors…and more importantly, in life. To be real honest, I wish I'd had one like it to read fifty years ago.

Robert H. Dedman Sr.
Dallas, Texas

Robert's Rules of Order

Rule #1
A sense of balance must apply to all areas of your life, not just your livelihood.

Rule #2
It's so important in life to have a life plan. Planning is a prelude to balance.

Rule #3
The more you learn, the more you earn. Even more importantly, the more you learn, the more you live.

Rule #4
A positive mental attitude is a key ingredient to a balanced, long, and happy life.

Rule #5
Humor is one of the best ways to get and keep a positive mental attitude. When times get tough, humor helps…even sick humor.

Rule #6
It's nice to be important, but even more important to be nice.

Rule #7
Setting up "win-win" relationships is the ultimate measure of success in life…and in business.

Rule #8
Be a giver, not a taker. They don't put luggage racks on hearses for good reason.

Rule #9
Integrity, good health, family, and friends are worth more than anything money can buy.

Rule #10
Don't forget to have fun. The more fun you have, the more money you make. It works both ways. The more money you make, the more fun you have.

GETTING READY

Robert's Rules of Order carry over and play off each other. They provide a balanced arsenal for daily living that's practically indestructible. Armed with the power they give you, you will be better able to recognize ways to fulfill your goals. When the time is right, you're ready. You go for it. Obviously, that's what happened to me. It's a shame when people live life part-time. They pursue happiness when they should strive for excellence. Happiness truly belongs to those who make excellence a habit.

1

Keeping Your Balance

You may be the world's greatest boss or your company's best manager, but if your spouse and family resent the inordinate amount of time you spend at the office, your personal life will suffer. If your children don't know their parents, if you can barely squeeze in time for exercise and other extracurricular activities, much less quality time with the ones you love, your biggest problem isn't work. It's probably balance. Your life is lop-sided. Your occupation has become your preoccupation.

That's why the first of Robert's Rules of Order is balance. You have to do more than pedal to ride a bicycle. You just can't concentrate on the traffic or the condition of the road ahead. You have to keep your balance to stay upright. This sense of balance applies to all aspects of your life, not just your livelihood. It must be a continuing goal to keep your total life in balance—your business life, civic life, social life, athletic life, church life, political life, family life, love life, sex life, etc. (And I usually interject into speeches that if the last three are all with the same person, it sure saves a lot of time.)

In the mid-1950s, I was trying to balance my work as an

attorney, build my own company, be a good husband, and help raise two children. So I'd take my son, Bob, with me to the office on weekends, just to spend some quality time with him in the car, office, and during lunch. What I didn't realize at the time was that he was learning to think like a businessman while I was striving for balance. I think he was five years old when one of our ClubCorp executives asked him what he wanted to be when he grew up. Bob said, "I'd like to be a businessman and play business like my daddy. He has a chair with wheels on the bottom. Mr. Poole (Richard Poole is a 38-year executive ClubCorp employee partner) has a chair with wheels on the bottom. I'll have a chair with wheels on the bottom and we'll all play business and make decisions."

Years later, it was déjà vu all over again with my grandson Jonathan. I've spent a lot of time with him playing golf and tennis or just taking him with me, wherever. When he was five years old, I was chairman of the Texas Highway Commission and pushed hard to extend the North Dallas Tollway. Once it was completed, I was given a lifetime pass to drive on it free as an act of gratitude by the Turnpike Authority. All I had to do was yell out "Number One" as I drove through the tollbooth. Well, Jonathan loved to crawl across the front seat of the car and yell, "Number One."

That was a pretty big deal to a five-year-old kid. So when someone asked Jonathan what he wanted to be when he grew up, he said, "I want to be a businessman like my Granddaddy and own the tollway." His perception apparently was that the Tollway was a real money machine with people driving by all day long, every day, throwing money into the toll basket. And he thought that I must own it because I was "Number One" and never had to pay the toll.

∾

Success is a journey, not a destination. Even if I'd never built ClubCorp, I still think I'd have been a success in this life. I might have picked another vehicle that didn't turn out as well or perhaps one that could have turned out even better. But I probably wouldn't have had nearly as much fun, and I might not have gotten as rich. But one thing's for sure—I was ready for whatever. I was looking around, thinking, planning, and getting the educational tools to be successful. As Henry Ford said, "Before everything else, getting ready is the secret of success."

The late James Michener was famous for his writing, but I latched onto something he said once at a college commencement speech. He said he felt that he had been a very lucky person all his life, but he thought luck was one of those things that was out there waiting for everybody. "If you're prepared when luck comes by, maybe you'll connect," he told the students. His challenge to them was "to do the hard work, be ready, and you and luck will come together."

The words of a few great poets spoke best to me about achieving balance in life. I'll share some of those poems with you throughout this book. Who knows? Some of them may speak to you as well. Rudyard Kipling's poem "If" first caused me to think in terms of balancing life and budgeting time. The poem is lengthy, but I will recite some parts that are relevant and most meaningful to me. *"If you can keep your head when all about you are losing theirs and blaming it on you,/ If you can trust yourself when all men doubt you,/ But make allowance for their doubting too."* When I'd be in tough corners and people would be pointing fingers at me, be it in business, clubs, politics, or just life in general, I'd contemplate these lines. When everybody would be going in different directions, I'd try to keep my equanimity by repeating Kipling's words of wisdom in my head. *"If you can dream—and not make dreams your master;/ If you can think—and not make thoughts your aim,/ If you can meet with Triumph and Disaster/ And treat those two impostors just the same.*" That's all about balance: not getting overly elated by your victories or overly dejected by your defeats. In other words, keep your balance and hold onto your equanimity.

Poetry that endures is the accumulated wisdom of the ages, expressed beautifully, succinctly and memorably, or it wouldn't endure. Most poetry that endures also has a God, man, duty, better-self theme running through its lines, like Ralph Waldo Emerson's "Voluntaries," which says, "*So nigh is grandeur to our dust,/ So near is God to man,/ When Duty whispers low, Thou must,/ The youth replies, I can.*" That theme just has a way of working on the psyche and helps keep everything in life in perspective. These lines have helped me remember that I have a duty to God and to myself as well as to my country, company, and family. Balancing professional and family demands is one of the most delicate tasks in life. Add in time to develop yourself as an individual and in relationship with God, and you indeed have a balancing challenge. But the rewards are yours for the taking later if you've lived a balanced life.

There are two other excerpts about balance in Kipling's poem that provide equally essential guideposts in life. "*If you can talk with crowds and keep your virtue,/ Or walk with Kings—nor lose the common touch.*" It's incredibly important not to get too self-centered or too impressed with yourself. You always need to be able to "walk with kings" and still keep the common touch. I think this is why I like to tell—and tell so many—jokes, and sometimes, a risqué one or two. It helps everyone, especially me, keep a balanced outlook on life. Like this well-worn tale of the rich old man who marries a beautiful young woman. After about a year of marital bliss, he says to her, "Sweetheart, if I lost all my money, would you still love me?" She says, "Of course, I would, honey, but I'd sure miss you."

☙

My wife Nancy has been instrumental in keeping our lives—together and individually—in balance ever since we met. I still remember our first meeting as if it were yesterday, although it was actually the fall of 1951. We were both attending the wedding reception of some mutual friends. The event was held at a large two-story house on Walnut Hill Lane, less than a mile from where we now live in Dallas. I spoke to Nancy during an encounter at the dining room table, which was set up buffet-style. She looked adorable and was drawing a big crowd of admirers when I joined in the conversation. Nancy, to this day, says it was love at first sight. I, too, was smitten and enjoyed getting to know her better that day.

Coincidentally, I already knew her very pretty roommate, Jayne Hodge. We were dating occasionally when Nancy and I met. Jayne was a stewardess, as we called flight attendants back then, for Braniff Airlines and, of course, always on the go. Nancy worked as a secretary for the chief geologist at Atlantic Richfield, one of the bigger oil companies in Dallas at the time. Actually, a co-worker of Nancy's had wanted to introduce her to me. As luck would have it, I was introduced to her roommate first. One night, I called and asked if Jayne was there. Nancy said she was off on a trip. I remember saying, "Well, would you like to go to a movie or something?" She said yes.

We started going together after that first date. A good friend of ours, Louis Turbeville, began dating Jayne and we four double-dated quite a bit. Louis and Jayne married sometime after we did. They were in our wedding and we were in theirs. Children came along and we all remained friends for years. Then, Louis died suddenly of a heart attack jogging, just a day after we had had a great time playing tennis at our home on Sunday afternoon. Now, years later, Jayne is married to a super guy named Ace Black and together, they make a very handsome couple. We see them from time to time, play golf on occasion, and they're both good friends of ours. Having such long-lasting friendships contributes to the balance and enjoyment of our lives.

❧

Ever since we said "I do," our schedules, individually and as a family, have been demanding but never boring. Our marriage has been based on the quality of time we're together. Skillful balancing has played a big part in bringing more than quantity to the time we do share with each other, and with our children and, now, grandchildren. What's more, we're like bookends. She likes to cook. I love to eat. We both like to plan. We revel in organization. If we're taking a trip, we're not apt to strike out with knapsacks on our backs. We're more prone to have it all mapped out and arranged for before we ever leave home. We spend a lot of time with important people, but we keep the common touch. We share a very good understanding of each other's importance, and try not to take advantage of anybody else. We're both reasonably cerebral, share similar values, and we love to laugh. I think it takes all those things, and more, to learn how to live and let live...and forgive. That thought reminds me of a one-liner about staying married: "The best secret to a lasting marriage is having realistic expectations and a poor memory."

I've always enjoyed this one, which emphasizes my point. A couple who've been married for fifty years are sharing a quiet moment in their rocking chairs on the front porch. The husband says, "Honey, would you make me an ice cream sundae with chocolate sauce and nuts and a cherry on top?" About ten minutes later, she comes back with a breakfast plate of bacon and eggs. He says, "Honey, I told you that you should have let me write it down for you. You forgot the toast." As Nancy's sister's mother-in-law in Oklahoma says, in a toast she occasionally gives: "Here's to the things to remember. Here's to the things to forget. And here's to the things to remember to forget."

It was my good fortune to encounter a delightful, well-educated, highly-principled and very feminine woman who became my wife. Fortunately, she thought I was adorable and I thought she was adorable—and still do. I lucked out and have managed to stay married for forty-five years. That speaks for itself—and for us. Maybe it's appropriate that our birthdays are interestingly matched, as well. Hers is February 13, mine is February 15. We "sandwich" Valentine's Day.

∾

Together, we raised super kids, who have a work ethic and a good sense of values. Wealth can make that more difficult, however. When asked why he had never had children, George Eastman, founder of Eastman Kodak Company, replied, "Because being as wealthy as I am, if I'd shared a lot of the wealth with them, it would have ruined them. And having it myself and not sharing it with them would have caused them to hate me." His wealth had put him on the horns of a dilemma about having children. I've noticed, however, that some of the wealthiest people who have garnered the balance and values in life also raise super children. That was the case for the Hunts, the Murchisons, the Clementses, the Corrigans, the O'Donnells, and the Perots in Dallas; the Bass families, both in Dallas and in Fort Worth; the Waltons in Arkansas; and the Fuquas in Georgia. These families created huge fortunes and raised super kids.

Nancy and I find great happiness in our two children. Patty and Bob are super kids in every way. Neither of them has ever been dependent on drugs or alcohol. They're both happily married and have great value systems. That's not something, I think, that just happened by chance. Nancy and I worked at it. We realized that children spend more time with and are primarily raised and influenced by their peer groups and teachers. Their peer groups are their contemporaries and their size, so they collaborate. Their parents are bigger and authoritarian and so, almost automatically, are identified as the enemy. We felt that if their peers smoked, our kids would have more of a propensity to smoke. If their peers did drugs, they would have been under more pressure to participate and possibly gang up against "the establishment." In other words, us.

So Nancy and I made a very conscious decision to spend as much time as we could with our kids. This often was difficult because of the number of commitments they already had. Dance lessons. Swimming lessons. Baseball games. Football practice. Tennis matches. You name it, our kids were involved. We countered that interference by taking them somewhere every chance we got, every vacation period they had, and spending sixteen hours a day with our kids. The object was to enjoy them and maybe even get them away from their peer groups and teacher groups who may or may not have been teaching them the values that we wanted them to learn.

When Bob and Patty were small, we stayed closer to home in Texas, with vacations focused on nearby places such as Oklahoma and Mexico. As they got older, we'd take longer trips during holiday breaks from school and month-long trips every summer. By the time they were both ten years old, they'd been to Europe once or twice. We took them on an around-the-world trip when Bob was thirteen. We still have pictures of him surrounded at the dinner table by pretty Thai girls with rosebud lips who helped us celebrate his thirteenth birthday in Bangkok. On one of those longer trips, we had a super time traveling to Hong Kong, India, Beirut, and Copenhagen, then back through Europe to the United States. The next year, we took them to Russia and Scandinavia, which provided profound learning experiences for them. In that cold-war era, no one in Russia seemed to smile. The "amenities" in hotels were not what we were used to at home. The water was brown and the towels were small and ragged with holes in them. The elevators and air conditioning seldom worked. I remember one morning when our breakfast consisted of only cucumbers and raw eggs. Finally, we got some hard rolls and coffee. It was an eye-opening experience for the children to see such a contrast to living conditions in the United States and such unhappy, depressed people who never smiled or laughed.

Those travels also gave them their "own head." When Patty and Bob got off the boat from Russia in Finland, they dropped to their knees and kissed the ground. The experiences taught them to do their own thinking, and of course, that's what Nancy and I intended. We hoped that they wouldn't be overly inclined to follow their peer groups into booze, drugs, or other misbehavior because they had learned lessons firsthand. They could never be enthralled by a planned economy which in reality becomes a political economy. No one could cloud their minds with communism or socialism because they'd seen it all in person. The best part was that we got to enjoy them in the process. Anytime you can spend sixteen hours a day with your children on a plane, train, boat, car, bus, or van, do it. You get to see the world through their eyes and they will see it through yours. The time together presents a special opportunity to inculcate good thought processes without preaching. You don't need to preach when you're seeing the world through each other's eyes. One trip alone included stops in Egypt, Israel, Jordan, Syria, Iraq, and Lebanon. We made other trips, to Tahiti, Australia, New Zealand, and the Fiji and South Seas Islands, also to Central and South America, and all over Africa. By the time Bob was twenty, I'm sure that he'd been to nearly every country in the world. And our trip around the world was probably the equivalent of a year's education because we saw so many different things, learned so many things, and acquired an appreciation for other countries and cultures. International travel definitely gave the children a respect for foreign cultures, other languages, and different ways of doing things. And it all helped them develop a sense of balance in their own lives.

❧

Our efforts to teach our children to be independent thinkers especially paid off when they went to high school, at the time when the schools in Dallas were being integrated. As Patty was entering the ninth grade, Nancy was fearful there'd be too much turmoil for her to get a good education. Although we'd been completely pleased with the public schools, Nancy thought it might be time to switch to private schools. Patty, however, became an eloquent spokesperson for staying in public schools. One day, she and her girlfriends cornered me in our bedroom to tell me that they thought they could help others adjust to the transition because they were leaders in their class. She told me that we'd always taught her to have absolutely no prejudice and to be leaders, and that she and Bob both felt they could do a great deal in helping to effect the transition. She also said she felt going to public schools was healthier than going to a private girls' school. She'd be too sheltered. It'd be much healthier to learn how to dress in regular clothes and not uniforms and how to get along with boys while she had us to help her, instead of waiting until she went off to college. Now that was an argument that would register between any father and his daughter. Nancy and I listened to and finally agreed with Patty, but regrettably, that first year of integration, with its busing and other tensions, turned out to be an unpleasant experience for both of our kids. They both eventually transferred to private school. No matter the circumstances, Patty has always expressed an incredible joy of living. Her teacher said one time, "Mr. Dedman, you must understand Patty doesn't just come into the room. She *descends* on the room."

❧

There's no substitute for parents spending time with their children. It seemed natural that Nancy spent more time with Patty and I spent more time with Bob. They did "girl stuff;" we did "boy stuff." There was one father-son program that was scheduled after work every week. We got involved in the Indian Guide program that revolved around building a bond between fathers and their sons. The kids couldn't even attend if their fathers didn't come. Their mothers couldn't substitute. I never missed a meeting. There were about eight or nine kids, all about nine years old, in the group. I remember we'd sit in the meetings with bands around our heads and feathers stuck in them. Bob was Little Running Bear and I was Big Running Bear. Part of the program was to go on camp-outs every once in a while. At the time, I thought, "Boy, whoever conceived this program had a good idea because it forces the father to spend time with the child." The dad had to rearrange his schedule to accommodate the activities. He couldn't afford to disappoint his son who would be pepped up about going to this meeting with his buddies and his dad and be with other dads and their sons. It was brilliantly conceived and served as a genuine bonding process between Bob and me.

Bob had a bad break befall him when he was about nine years old. He developed a disease called Legg-Perthés, meaning the top of his hip bone didn't get enough blood supply so it got soft and caused him pain. The only cure for it at that time was to take a sling over his shoulder, put it around his foot and lift it up off the ground behind his back. With this contraption, he couldn't put his foot on the ground for two years while the disease overcame itself and his hip strengthened so he could walk. Even though he had to have this sling holding his leg up behind his back and use crutches, we didn't let it slow us down taking him places. When things got too tough, we'd get a wheelchair and push. It was critical for such a growing boy, from ages nine to eleven, to retain his independence even though he couldn't run and play like the other kids. As parents, we had to maintain a delicate balance. We felt sorry for him, but we couldn't feel too sorry for him. He still had to grow into a man even if he was sick. He'd even take on his mother in tennis on crutches and sometimes win. You'd never know this history to observe him today. He's done incredibly well.

∾

We taught the kids about the balance between fiscal responsibility and the value of money. We gave Patty our old Fleetwood Cadillac when she was sixteen that we'd had for three or four years. We figured that was the safest car she could drive because it was like a tank. It wasn't too fancy like a sports car that she might try to race or show off in. When Bob turned sixteen we gave him a large, old clunker of ours, for the same reasons. It was like a tank, too. I thought it might help him be a bit more conservative in his driving. I was wrong, sort of. When he drove over a lawn in North Dallas, the homeowner got the license plate number and called me. I told Bob he needed to personally apologize to the gentleman and fix the ruts in his yard, which he dutifully did. We never had that kind of problem again. I do remember, however, that Bob wanted a new car of his own instead of that old clunker. So he volunteered to get himself in shape, trim down, and make straight A's if I would buy him a new car. He handed me a document that said, "This is to certify my dad has agreed to buy me a car of my choice, not to exceed $14,000 U.S. (hard evidence of his knowledge of the world)." I signed it. He signed it. He lived up to his end of the bargain and so did I. He got his new car.

∾

You can coach more by positives than by negatives. The more you praise somebody for doing something right, the more he or she will continue to do other things right and become role models for others. My motto is: "Always praise in public, and coach in private." I try to do some praising of people in public in every way I can every day—generally because I think they deserve it, but also because I think it motivates them to do better. I remember once when we bought a club, we noticed something very wrong before we ever walked in the door. The key employees had reserved parking spaces near the front door of the clubhouse. We gave those preferred spaces to the members overnight, and moved our staff's cars to a parking lot somewhat farther away. We made that change swiftly and efficiently, but without hurting anybody's feelings. We explained the change as simply a part of demonstrating our "member-first" philosophy. Obviously, it went over big with our members.

As for coaching I've done in private, if I gave you an example, it wouldn't be private anymore.

For me, the "sandwich technique" has always worked well in talking to our employee partners about something that needs to be addressed. I'll first tell them what a good job they're doing, and then visit with them about some of the things that could be improved. Then I conclude by telling them of my respect for them, how much better they are going to do, and assuring them that I'm only a phone call away if I can help them in any way. This technique works because people hear me. They don't have time to jump on the defensive and quit listening. Remember this: If you criticize before they know you're on their side, they won't hear anything you say. They're too busy thinking, "Oh, gosh, he doesn't like me" or "Oh, no, he thinks what I'm doing is not good." I've been more successful by starting positively about something they're doing right before I talk about something they could do better. Then I try to end the conversation on a positive note by encouraging them to do better because I know they can.

A man named Chuck Bishop was my first hire at Brookhaven Country Club when we first went into the club business. He became quite familiar with my sandwich technique. After we had been partners for several years, he said, "Bob, cut out all this sandwich crap. We've been friends long enough that I know your technique and use it myself. So if you have something to say, get with it. You don't have to worry so much about hurting my feelings. I know you know we're partners and we butter our bread on the same side." Well, after about six months of my being more direct, he had another request. He said, "Bob, would you mind going back to that sandwich technique again?"

A good manager has to have attributes like a good minister. You have to maintain a delicate balance, knowing when to "comfort the afflicted" and when to "afflict the comfortable" and how much of both is enough. Once, while trying to teach and influence one of our people who was perhaps a little too comfortable at the time, I said, "Do you realize that you and I have something in common?" He said, "What's that, Bob?" I said, "You and I both have probably gone as high in this company as we're ever going to." Well, he was visibly shaken. Even though I immediately told him that I was just joking, my point had been made. I had "afflicted the comfortable," albeit in a sensitive and humorous manner, then I put my arm around him and gave him a big hug and told him how proud I was to be his partner.

∾

Anybody in business is really in the "people mechanics" business. You have to be a practicing industrial psychologist without the benefit of a license. You must be able to assess people, to read them, to judge their long and short suits. You need to be able to recruit and retain them and organize them into a good team. Then you have to motivate them to do as good as they know how to do, and then coach them to be better than they know how to be and to be the best they can be. And you must be able to keep numerical, not adjectival, score on how well you're doing. You have to keep score, as opposed to using some meaningless adjective like, "Oh, we're doing well," or "better" or "worse." I'm very numerically oriented to have preciseness of thought and communication, and so is my son. Suppose I asked you, "What did you shoot in golf today?" You might say, "Well, pretty good," or "Not so good," or "Not as good as I should have." That forces me into an assessment mode. What standards did your parents instill in you? What is your perception of good or bad? But if you just give me one number, if you say, "I shot 120," then I have a very good idea of how you hit your woods and your irons and your putts. But if you say, "I shot 71," I still have a very good idea and instant communication. Ernest Hemingway once wrote: "Do not confuse movement with action." I agree. I also think that people often confuse chatter with communication. Too much chatter really means no one's listening.

❧

There's another aspect of balance—of symmetry in life—that we all can look in a mirror and see. God gave everyone two ears and one mouth as a coaching device to listen more and talk less. Think of it as a nudge to always listen twice as much as you talk. The secret is to listen to someone else until they agree with you. That's the best technique for being a good salesperson. Some people think you've got to be glib and chatty and overpower somebody with a lot of words. But that's just the opposite of what you ought to do. Many times, the best question to ask is, "What do you want?" If you can give it to somebody, you can set up a productive relationship for both partners—and make the sale. I don't know of an organization, ours included, that doesn't depend on a salesperson to make it go.

Every company's chairman of the board has to be a salesperson. He or she might have started out as an engineer or a lawyer or an accountant, but his or her rise to the top is in direct proportion to his or her sales ability. Some people might have fancier titles now like chief executive officer or chief operating officer, but those at the top are the company's best salespeople. Or they don't reach the top. My vision for ClubCorp has always been based on service and sales. To this day, I list "salesman" on my passport, IRS forms, and other documents on which you have to state your occupation. People ask me, "You don't list attorney or executive?" Some have even suggested "philanthropist." No, I list salesman. I think everything begins with a sale. That's what makes the world go 'round. Sales make possible the income stream to hire the lawyers, architects, engineers, accountants, executives, and everyone else. Selling is a noble profession, and I always profess it with pride. Still, there are always a few who don't get it. They ask me, "You mean you went to college four-degrees-worth just to be a salesman?" And my answer is, "Yes, to be a *better* salesman." In fact, as chairman of the board, I believe I am my company's best salesman because I founded the company and set its vision on how to balance sales, service, and pricing to give the best value. There always has to be a balance between knowing what you can promise and what you can deliver. It is probably a tendency of salespeople to over-promise, while an active and informed chairman of the board knows it's important to avoid over-promising and then under-delivering.

When you want to bring someone else to your point of view and you are 180 degrees apart, the best thing to do is listen. The more you listen, the greater your chances become of finding out where the other person is coming from and possibly uncovering areas of agreement between the two of you. Remember, it's much easier to supplement someone's thinking than it is to supplant it. But you can't even supplement it if you don't know their thinking. The more you listen to someone else, the more they are inclined to listen to you.

Salesmanship

There is a definite technique to selling and perhaps a few tips will help you become a better salesperson for your company. Imagine you're in retail. It is not an effective selling technique to ask someone if they want to buy a shirt. Instead, ask, "Do you want the green shirt or the blue shirt?" That way, it's an either-or question that cannot be answered with a "yes" or a "no." If they pick green, you can obviously sell them that shirt . . . and maybe the blue one, too. Staying away from questions with yes or no answers is one of the best talents of a good salesperson. A wise haberdasher knows how to take advantage of a sale. After you've bought a suit from him, he might ask, "Do you want to buy a couple of ties to go with your new suit?" Or "do you want to accessorize your new suit with a couple of new shirts?" Or "do you need a pair of black shoes to go with your new suit?" Or "how about a new belt that would go with this suit better than the one you have on now?" Once someone is in a buying frame of mind, add-on sales are often easier to make than the first one. Selling is truly an art that people could study and be incredibly good at, if they'd just do it.

~

Balancing your time will make every aspect of your life richer. These thoughts take me back to Kipling's poem, which concludes: "*If you can fill the unforgiving minute/ With sixty seconds' worth of distance run/ Yours is the Earth and everything that's in it,/ And—which is more—you'll be a Man, my son!*" Those words inspired me to make every second count in life, to practice time management, to set goals, and to have a life plan. To have balance, you have to plan. To plan, your life must have balance. And to squeeze it all in, you constantly have to budget your time. But do these things, and you can have it all.

SPEAKING OF...

I was fifty years old the first time I ever gave my P-L-A-N speech. I was to receive the Entrepreneur of the Year award for Texas in 1976 and had to come up with a reasonably short, but meaningful, speech. I probably thought about it for about a week while shaving or showering in the mornings or driving somewhere during the day. Then, finally, about one or two days before the ceremony, I decided on the four-legged chair with a letter for each leg, P-L-A-N. The first time I used it, the "N" was for my wife Nancy. She was with me that day, and it was a nice thing to say because part of being married is caring and sharing and being nice. Later on, I changed the N to "be Nice" more as a practical matter. Not everybody has a wife named Nancy.

Abraham Lincoln was asked one time how long it took him to prepare a speech. He said, "Well, it depends on how long the speech is. If it's a five-minute speech, it'll take me two weeks. If it's a twenty-minute speech, it'll take me a week. If it's an hour speech, I'm ready now." That advice has helped me plan and be prepared.

2

Okay, Now Here's the P-L-A-N

I don't think I was quite eighteen years old when a cartoon made an indelible impression on me. Two old men with long beards were locked away in a dungeon, their bare feet shackled to the wall. Cobwebs and rats surrounded them. Their clothes were tattered and torn. Their hair and beards were white and straggly. Their bodies were emaciated. It was obvious that they'd been in this desperate plight for some time. The caption under the cartoon was one man saying to the other, "Okay, now here's the plan." I immediately recognized the humor of that cartoon, yet realized the wisdom in its caption. And I have never forgotten its truth. As long as you have a plan and a positive mental attitude, you're never whipped. No matter what. You see the problems. You believe in your ability to solve them, and you make a plan. You can turn adversity into advantage, and lemons into lemonade.

I frequently travel around the country, especially around graduation time, talking about "A P-L-A-N for Life." My only prop is a four-legged chair. Most people think about sitting down when they see a chair. I think about standing up and giving a speech. I name each of the chair's legs, P-L-A-N. The "P" stands for Planning, "L" for Learning, "A" for positive mental Attitude, and "N" stands for be Nice. I enlist the aid of a four-legged chair because just looking at it shows the importance of balance better than I could possibly explain. If any of its legs are out of balance, the chair (and the person sitting in it) comes tumbling down—regardless of how well you've cared for the other three legs. The talk is about keeping your life in balance. But the first leg on the chair stands for "Planning" because I believe planning is a prelude to balance.

It's so important in life to have a life plan. I had one by the time I was eighteen, inspired by the incredibly humble circumstances of my childhood in Rison, Arkansas. Born in 1926, just before the Great Depression, I was the first of four children of Robert H. and Cornelia Worsham Dedman. I often describe our parents as being "too poor to paint and too proud to whitewash." But they also had an enlightened attitude that the best place to find a helping hand was at the end of your own arm. They believed, as Henry Ford was quoted, "Chop your own wood, and it will warm you twice." Our parents raised us in a strong spirit of self-help, regardless of what town or conditions in which we were living. So that combination of poverty, pride, and a self-help attitude gave me an inordinate desire to succeed and extricate myself from those cotton fields in south central Arkansas.

ॐ

In truth, I had two different families: I came first, then Phil two years later, and then Linda and Smitty. My youngest brother and sister were born much later and grew up together. Phil and I shared more of our growing up, but drifted apart over the years, especially after I went into the Navy and studied at various colleges, while Phil joined the Marine Corps. He died several years ago of emphysema. Linda and Smitty still live in Rison and are retired. Smitty divides his time among golf, hunting, and fishing. Linda, who once helped shape young minds as a schoolteacher, has a grown son, Paul Scarborough, who is now in law school.

Most of my childhood took place during the Depression. That will mean something to some of you; to others, it won't. Indoor plumbing was something extraordinary back then for many people in rural and smaller communities, including us. Although I didn't view my family as richer or poorer than anyone else's, we were poorer than most. We moved frequently, depending upon where my father could find work. I can even remember moving simply because we couldn't pay the rent. We moved to Tyler when I was four years old and lived in a brick house, as I recall. I had the mumps there and that's about all I remember about Tyler the first time around. When I was either four or five, we moved to Lindale. Dad got a job at a Ford car dealership there. I think he probably had a job at a dealership in Tyler, but for some reason, he felt it would be cheaper and maybe better to live and raise his sons in Lindale. We lived there about a year before I started the first grade.

Even as a kid, I was never allergic to work…or school. I did have some trouble, though, with our black pig Ikie and about forty white leghorn chickens always trying to follow me to school or a neighbor's house in Lindale. We raised Ikie from a little bitty baby pig. I fed him enough slop from the house once or twice a day that he grew big enough for me to ride around the yard. Ultimately, though, we ate him.

We also raised the chickens from little baby chicks at the same time. We put them in big cardboard boxes with a light bulb for warmth. I fed them once or twice a day and picked up their eggs when they became hens. We couldn't afford a dog or cat, so these animals became like pets. I'd be around them during the day and we were just close friends. When they'd follow me, my friends' mothers would ask me to send the pig and the chickens back home. They didn't want them to mess up their yards.

After we moved to Tyler the second time, I came down with double pneumonia and a ruptured appendix at the same time. I was around nine years old. Even so, I remember being packed in ice as if the doctors were trying to freeze me. I guess they were trying to lessen the pneumonia before they operated on my appendix. Whatever their motivation, it did rupture and I damn near died. With body temperatures over 106 degrees, I hallucinated about monsters that came out of lamps and pieces of furniture. I still remember their hideous faces.

If you're like me, you're not terribly impressed with those vanity books where people go on and on interminably about themselves. But I do think there are things that happen to you as a kid that help shape the adult you become. This is what I'm trying to accomplish by telling you about my childhood. Looking back as a grown man, it's much easier to see how the pieces fit together to complete the puzzle. The fact we moved around a lot, I think, contributed a great deal to my desire for success. Constantly losing old friends and having to make new ones. Adjusting to new surroundings. Getting sick and finding out that I was stronger than I ever imagined. Adjusting to different schools, but still able to make good grades. Dealing with the inside politics of each community and the different personalities of people who lived there. Figuring out how to get ahead in a place where I was usually a stranger. I'm sure that it all influenced the adult personality that I later acquired. It fueled my passion for planning as well as my propensity for lofty goals.

∾

I've been goal-setting my entire life. However, it's my humble opinion that only 20 percent of the people really have clearly-defined goals, written down, and thought through, that say, "This is what I want to achieve in my life." Only about 20 percent of that group have clearly-defined plans on how to achieve those goals. And what's worse, only about 20 percent of that group will make the commitment to work the plan to achieve their goals. So when you have only 20 percent of 20 percent of 20 percent of the people who have clearly-defined goals and plans and commitments to achieve them, you really have only about .8 of 1 percent of the people—which is probably about the number of people who are super-achievers. I think it's important in all organizations that you communicate clearly where you're trying to go and how you plan to get there, so everyone will know his or her role as a team player. ClubCorp does an incredible amount of planning and it pays off. But be forewarned, the process takes a concerted effort. In our company, we believe you have to plan your work.

∾

Making money has always been one of my goals...even as a kid. We moved to Dallas when I was ten and in the fifth grade. The best part about that move was my paper route that included the Melrose Hotel off Cedar Springs, one of the most opulent hotels at the time—and a place to see and be seen. It was exciting to me to view the comings and goings of well-known "movers and shakers" of the day and I imagined that some day I would be part of this world. On a more practical note, the paper route provided what I considered pretty good money, which I used to mainly buy food, maybe a new pair of blue jeans to wear, and other electives...like shoes.

We moved back to Rison when I was twelve. I picked huckleberries in the spring and cotton in the summer, although the latter mostly under protest. You see, cotton fields are dusty and miserable when the weather is dry. Winds blow the dirt around and it collects on the cotton. When there's rain, the ground was soggy and muddy, but I always welcomed the opportunity to make more money per hour. After all, we were paid by the pound and the damp cotton weighed more. Thinking back, it was pretty hard to find a comfortable time to pick cotton. I preferred huckleberries. They would bring 35 cents for a gallon of black ripe ones and 25 cents for a mixture of red and green ones. It would take most of a day to pick one or two gallons, but you have to remember, full wages for a grown, able-bodied man at that time were 50 cents a day, and a worker felt lucky to get them. Huckleberries were a big deal because of the money we could get for them.

Interestingly enough, legendary football coach Bear Bryant and I hail from the same part of Arkansas. I wouldn't be surprised if he, too, picked a huckleberry or two. I read a story about him one time in *Sports Illustrated* magazine. He said, "People always said I had a lot of intensity and drive. It's because I wanted to do good enough that I never had to go back to those Moro bottoms in south central Arkansas." The same motivation drove me. I didn't want to go back. So part of me really didn't mind when, in 1940, hard times forced my parents to send my younger brother Phil and me to live with our widowed aunt in Dallas. At fourteen, I started the ninth grade at North Dallas High School. That's where my perhaps unlikely fascination with poetry began.

ॐ

Words of great poets like Emerson, Kipling, Browning, and Longfellow inspired me and my passion for pursuing my life's dreams—they also went straight to my heart. Poetry became the umbilical cord for my positive mental attitude and nurtured my heartfelt inspiration to do good for others. In fact, I now look back on those formative years with some amazement that I was so attentive to their wisdom at that early age. Some poetry, I discovered on my own. Much of it, I memorized as part of my schoolwork at the insistence of Ms. Bertrand, my high school teacher who taught me a ton about English. I owe her, in part, for my discovery of the insights that led to my being successful in life...and in business. In poetry I even found messages that inspired me to develop such a work ethic that I've never complained about working hard. Hard work has always been good for me, and to me.

Another favorite poem is "Rabbi Ben Ezra," written by Robert Browning for his wife, Elizabeth Barrett Browning. He could see that she was getting a bit concerned about aging, so he wrote a birthday poem of sorts: "*Grow old along with me!/ The best is yet to be,/ The last of life, for which the first was made:/ Our times are in His hand/ who saith "A whole I planned,/ Youth shows but half; trust God: see all nor be afraid!"* This poem made me think in terms of life planning. I was silly if I didn't plan for my whole life, instead of just part of it. Sam Walton, founder of Wal-Mart and one of my all-time role models, was quoted as saying: "I believe in always having goals, and always setting them high." Sam and I were alike in that regard. I realized two things in trying to set up a life plan to achieve my goals. The first was, by and large, that people who made the most money worked the hardest. People who worked forty hours a week or less usually worked for people who worked sixty hours a week or more. And the people who worked sixty hours a week or more, made more per hour because they learned more and tackled bigger commitments. And since they worked one-and-a-half times as long as their subordinates and were paid more per hour as bosses, they made almost twice as much money. More important, they had less time to spend their money. That gave them the ability to accumulate and invest their earthly resources, and get a geometric multiplicand going for themselves.

Kipling's poem "If" led me to think not only in terms of balance but also time-budgeting. When he talked about filling the *"unforgiving minute,"* I thought about the fact that there are 168 hours in a week. I figured, if I set aside 56 hours to sleep, I still have 112 waking hours. That's a lot of time. If I invested up to 80 hours in gainful endeavors, I would still have 32 hours left to do with whatever my heart desires. To dance, to play golf or tennis, to go to church, to make love, to do whatever. I determined that, God willing, I could expect to live to be eighty years old. So I set up a life plan to work 80 hours a week from the time I was twenty until age thirty-five, then taper off to 60-hour weeks from thirty-five to age fifty, then to 40-hour weeks from fifty to age sixty-five, and 20-hour weeks from sixty-five on. If all was going well, from sixty-five on, I'd either goof off or be a scalawag or do whatever else lazy people do.

I had a clearly-defined goal and a time commitment for achieving it on a weekly basis. I had a life plan, a sixty-year plan, fifteen-year plans, five-year plans, one-year plans, and weekly time-budgeting plans. They were all important, and I lived up to the expectations I imposed upon myself. Now you still might be thinking that putting in 80 hours a week at work doesn't leave enough time for enjoying life. I think it does and here's why: Whatever you do in life, do it to the hilt. If you enjoy it, you'll do better. The hours you put into your vocation aren't really work if you enjoy it. I found I could put in long hours, not get tired, and feel fulfilled. If you're not enjoying what you're doing, you can work forever and still not make good money. The bottom line is that you won't enjoy life if you don't like your work. It's absolutely essential to find something that fits and allows you to feel a sense of nobility. I liken this sense to the story about two bricklayers. Someone asked one what he was doing, and he said, "I'm making $14 an hour." When the second one was asked the same question, he replied, "I'm building a cathedral." Obviously, the one with the sense of nobility about what he was doing wasn't working at all. He was having a ball. That's how I feel about my work.

Larry King, the late-night talk show host, said something along these lines after his heart attack in 1987: "I thought if I was lucky enough to live, I'd change myself. I realized I could have a new life—new energy, new endurance and feel better about myself." And Will Rogers, a talker in his own right, once offered this advice: "If you want to be successful, it's just this simple. Know what you are doing. Love what you are doing. And believe in what you are doing." I couldn't agree more.

෴

My goal included getting rich while living a balanced life. That life plan that I had by age eighteen was very specific. I wanted to make $50 million—and be giving away at least $1 million a year—by the time I was fifty. Yet having goals isn't enough. You must have workable, realistic plans to achieve those goals. By the time I was twenty-three in 1949, my plan was progressing. I was a partner in my own law firm—Shank, Dedman, and Payne—in Dallas. I attended Southern Methodist University in Dallas at night to earn my master's degree in law, while building a successful law practice with an excellent track record. And one of our clients, H.L. Hunt, was developing a widespread reputation for making money—roughly $1 million a week. As a wildcatter of legendary proportions drilling oil and gas wells, he was thought to be the wealthiest man in the world at the time.

Maybe we should backtrack for a moment. Admittedly, not many twenty-three-year-olds are partners in their own law firms, not to mention having clients such as Mr. Hunt. While I was going to law school, I had full-time jobs selling insurance during the week and selling real estate on the weekends. I would sit on houses that were for sale and, between clients, I would study. As I recollect, I was making more than a thousand dollars a month, which was good money in those days, especially for anyone going to law school full-time. About that time, one of my professors had written a prominent Dallas attorney, Ralph Shank, to tell him about my engineering degree, a helpful credential for an oil and gas attorney. His letter also spoke of my entrepreneurial efforts in insurance and real estate. Mr. Shank wrote back, saying that I was making more money than I could expect to make for a long time in the legal profession, but if I decided to be a lawyer, to call him.

After graduation, I seized an opportunity to be a "law-gineer" for a large construction company in San Antonio. I wore khakis three days a week as an engineer and suits three days a week as a lawyer. I also set up an insurance agency for the company so that we could write policies on the homes, apartments, and shopping centers we were building. It was a good life, and I was making good money. Still, it didn't take me long to realize I was not going to get rich building houses. So I decided to move to Dallas and revive the contact with Ralph Shank. I just walked into his office and introduced myself. Mr. Shank and I had a good visit and made a partnership deal on the spot. He had a couple of vacant offices and had already made a deal with Bob Payne, who was just getting out of law school, so we set up the law firm of Shank, Dedman, and Payne and commenced business on October 1, 1949. I remember my starting draw was only $200 a month.

Mr. Hunt was a stepping stone for me because of what I learned while working with him. He believed that possession was nine-tenths of the law and that at least 90 percent of the time, the owner in possession could sign a valid lease. So his "lease hounds" didn't do nearly as much title search work as those from other companies. That meant Mr. Hunt's men could out-lease others, generally by a factor of about ten to one in a lease play in a new hot area. He obviously would flange up the title on a tract before he would drill on it. But this aggressive approach naturally led to more litigation for him than for more conservative companies. Mr. Hunt was playing the percentages like a poker player, using litigation to shore up many titles. I quickly gained a reputation for winning an extraordinary number of these cases—something that caught Mr. Hunt's attention.

Mr. Hunt used to tell me, "I may not always have the best ideas in the world, but when I hear one, I'm able to recognize it, appropriate it, and adopt it as my own." I tucked away that advice. I learned to listen, learn from what I heard, and use what I saw work. Mr. Hunt was a good teacher. Although he did not graduate from high school, he was probably the most voracious reader and student of everything that life offers. As an oilman, he believed in hard work and analyzing every aspect he could about every reservoir. He was probably one of the most learned and analytical people—not just about oil reservoirs, but about everything—I have ever known. Like Michener, he also believed in luck as being part of his life's plan. For example, he noticed that nearly every one of his companies named with six-letter words and beginning with the letter "P" did incredibly well. Not one to mess with fate, he kept churning out company names that fit that formula...Penrod Drilling Company, Placid Oil Company, Parade Products, Panola Gas Systems, etc.

In addition, Mr. Hunt was probably the world's original naturalist. He pushed that philosophy quite hard and lived to a ripe old age with all of his faculties intact. His program was eating healthy foods that he had grown on his farms, from healthy soils and unadulterated by artificial fertilizers or herbicides or insecticides. He'd bring what he called his "healthy foods from healthy soils" lunch to the office every day in a brown paper sack. It was somewhat amusing when people were invited to have lunch with

Mr. Hunt. I'm sure most of them had visions of partaking in some sumptuous luncheon, but he'd take out his paper sack and start spreading out his rabbit-type food on the coffee table and graciously offer, "What would you like?" As he started munching on a carrot, you could almost see their faces visibly drop over such a low-key and healthy luncheon with the world's wealthiest man.

A Twist of the Wrist

During my early days of practicing law, I developed a habit, which I retain to this day, that attracted Mr. Hunt's notice. Whenever I went into an important meeting, I would turn my watch over on my wrist so I could keep tabs on the time and remind myself to mainly listen. Then I would do just that. After about 45 or 50 minutes, when I had heard the various points of view, I would finally speak, beginning, "It appears to me." Most often, the other people in the meeting would agree with me. This method is how I honed my decision-making technique of clearly defining the problem, the salient facts, alternative courses of action, and my recommended course of action. I was so successful in guiding groups to a conclusion that Mr. Hunt told his top executives to invite me to every meeting that involved more than a million dollars. And, I'd like to think that having a plan is partly how I won Mr. Hunt's trust. My relationship with him was one of the most extraordinary of my life.

Working to fulfill my life plan, I diligently observed Mr. Hunt's approach to being wealthy. Interestingly, he began devoting much of his waking energies toward saving the country and the world, as opposed to making more money. As his mouthpiece and general counsel, I became very involved in that process. In

1951, he set up a foundation called "Facts Forum" and appointed me as president. We went about our task by setting up small groups of people around the country who would meet and debate the issues of the day.

We lined up radio and television programs to air their debates on current issues that were updated every month. We had a show on the Liberty Broadcasting Network (the biggest radio network at the time), along with more shows on independent television stations than anybody else. There weren't any television networks then, so we had quite a national following and became a popular venue for the dissemination of ideas and public debate. Facts Forum became so well known that, after President Dwight Eisenhower was elected in 1952, he called us and wanted to get his Cabinet members on our programs to push some of his initiatives as a brand new president. We had shown that having a "P-L-A-N" was one of the best ways to reach grassroots America.

Even today, what we did isn't that different from public relations, for which, of course, I have a story. It takes place when Moses is leading the Israelites out of Egypt and comes up to the banks of the Red Sea with the Egyptian army in hot pursuit. He turns to his advisors and asks, "What shall we do?" His general says, "Let's fight." Moses says, "Goodness, we've lost every fight for four hundred years. That's the main reason we're leaving." Moses' attorney says, "Let's negotiate." Moses says, "Goodness, we've lost every negotiation for four hundred years. That's another reason we're leaving." So Moses turns to his P.R. man and asks, "What would you say if I waved my arms and the waters of the Red Sea opened and we go to the other side? The Egyptian army follows in hot pursuit and I wave my arms again, the sea closes and the army drowns in the waters as we stand safely on the other side." His P.R. man thinks a minute about it and says, "Moses, baby, you do that and I'll guarantee you two full pages in the Old Testament."

∾

The goal behind Facts Forum was pretty simple. Mr. Hunt figured that 95 percent of all radio and eventually television shows at the time were quite liberal and far to the left of center. He included in that group commentators and analysts who really controlled the airwaves, along with the editorial writers and front-page editors of major metropolitan newspapers. He believed America was being saturated with a far-left program, and his goal was for the country to have more balanced information—more of a fifty-fifty deal. His conservative view was that the basic wisdom of less government would prevail, if the best liberal could espouse his side and the best conservative—he actually called them "constructives"—could espouse the other side, resulting in a totality of views. In this manner, we might better adjust the balance between sides. So Facts Forum basically became a gigantic nationwide debating society with that goal in mind.

In fact, there were two specific goals that Mr. Hunt outlined for Facts Forum and that he expected me, as president, to reach. I learned much about planning in executing his campaign. Mr. Hunt's Number One goal was to achieve passage of the 22nd Amendment, which would limit the terms of the president. He was fearful that we wouldn't have free elections again if a liberal, like another Roosevelt, came along and dominated for a lengthy period. In his mind, such a president would appoint so many justices to the Supreme Court that the balance of power in the U.S. would go too far to the left side to ever recover. So we devised a platform that promoted a limit on the terms of the president, got it debated among Congress and members of the electorate, and the 22nd Amendment passed. I saw that Mr. Hunt's methodical approach worked...and I never forgot it.

Mr. Hunt's second goal was to get the terms "ecology" and

"environmentalism," through the avenue of Facts Forum, incorporated into the American vernacular. As already noted, Mr. Hunt was one of the world's most ardent supporters of environmental initiatives at the time. Very few people had ever heard the terms "ecology" and "environmentalism," much less understood their meanings or significance. So we would set up debates and ask questions like "Are we doing enough for our ecology?" or "Are we doing enough for environmentalism?" or "Are we doing enough reforestation?" I remember taking a certain amount of ribbing from members of the press for such questions. They'd ask, "What's this ecology rhetoric?" mainly because they didn't actually know themselves what the word meant. But Facts Forum sessions generated enough of a discussion that I credit the program with much of the reason that ecology, environmentalism, and reforestation are terms very much a part of today's lexicon.

Mr. Hunt also was one of the best in terms of calculating business probabilities—probably better than anyone else I've ever met or known. This skill is one of the reasons that he became so wealthy. It wasn't just luck. He worked at it. At that time, only about one in ten wildcat wells would "come in," or, in other words, produce oil. People trying to raise money to drill a well, such as syndicators or promoters, would say, "We'll get a three-to-one return on our money if the well hits." Obviously, when you only have one-in-ten chances of hitting and only get three-to-one recovery on your money when you do, it's just a matter of time before you go broke. Mr. Hunt wouldn't drill a prospect unless he felt his chances were infinitely greater in return potential than the prospects of hitting the well.

I studied his genius for calculating probabilities, and suspect that some of it came from his talent for playing poker. You may have heard others say never draw to an "inside straight," but you might not know why. Holding five cards that are sequential—a "straight"—is one of the higher winning hands in poker. So if you have two cards on the beginning of that straight and two cards on the end, there are only four cards that you could draw to complete that straight in the middle. But in draw poker, if you have four cards that are sequential in your hand and you could draw one card on either end of it, you'd have eight cards that you could draw to complete the straight and double the probability of drawing a winning card. I often use this as an example of the importance of calculating probabilities in playing cards, and in playing out your business plans. It's a lot like the 80-20 Rule. Usually, 20 percent of your deals makes 80 percent of your money. Twenty percent of your deals requires 80 percent of your time, effort, and energy. All smart business schools teach the 80-20 Rule. The longer I'm in business, the more I realize that it's really true.

～

At ClubCorp, we repeatedly preach truisms, like "Proper prior planning prevents pretty poor performance," "Plan the work and work the plan," "Plan for the very best, work for the very best, but plan for the worst, too," and "If you fail to plan, you are inadvertently planning to fail." ClubCorp has five-year plans, one-year plans, four-week plans, and one-week plans. We spend substantial time developing the plans, working them, and monitoring how well they work. Sometimes, however, even well-formulated plans have to change. People laughingly have said that CCA (ClubCorp of America) actually stands for "Change Corporation of America." That's okay. Plans are essential, but I don't think they require religious adherence. If a plan is working, stick with it. If it's not working, change it. In any football game, there's a game plan. If one team has more points on the scoreboard, that coach ought to stick with it. If the team is behind, the coach needs to regroup his players and learn from what didn't work…and from what did.

Probably the two biggest decisions I've made in pursuing my life plan were getting married and starting ClubCorp. At thirty-one, I had a perfect launch pad for my plan. I had long ago extricated myself from those cotton fields of south central Arkansas. I had four degrees and a successful law practice. I was married and had two young children. I was H.L. Hunt's general counsel and worked with him on many projects. But I was growing restless and felt the timing was right for a change of plans. I had become frustrated by the ever-increasing intervention of Big Government in the oil and gas industry, which was one of my specialty areas. I could see that being a lawyer had serious time, income, and income tax limitations. My goal of having a very successful personal life, while creating a profitable business life, needed a jump start. As an estate attorney, I discovered there was little opportunity to create much of my own estate. I found it increasingly tedious to counsel and cajole others to do something, watch them only partially follow my advice, and then hold me accountable for the results.

Interestingly, at this time, I did quite a bit of domestic relations work at our firm. I counseled our young clients on the necessity of planning that I myself had been practicing—and hoped to continue in the future. I would tell young people when they got married to bank the wife's earnings and try to live on just the husband's income. It's true that two can live more cheaply together than they can apart, especially if they have two incomes. But three can't live as cheaply as two, which is exacerbated if they only have one income. By living off the husband's income, they wouldn't get accustomed to living beyond their means, and have to give it all up when they started a family. When a baby's on the way, expenses usually go up and incomes often drop. Many marriages falter at that juncture. They may survive as a couple, but later succumb to harbored resentments over not being able to maintain the same standard of living. If they learn to live on one income, they don't have quite the same shock when they start to raise a family.

Even though times were good, my destiny was being determined by others and not by me. It's true, you know, until you decide that you are going to be in charge of your own destiny, your best efforts are little more than tinkering around in playing the game. I wanted to find a way to become a principal instead of just being an advisor. I began to use "my spare time" to look for a vehicle to get richer than I could practicing law. At thirty, I stumbled upon my destiny, as luck would have it, on a golf course in Rancho Mirage, California, near Palm Springs. I learned that a couple of golf pros had started Thunderbird Country Club in 1952 by buying up raw land for $2,000 per acre. In 1957, they were selling four lots per acre, for $50,000 a lot. This probably goes without saying, but I was greatly captivated with the "value added" of going from $2,000 to $200,000 an acre in five years. This land had increased in value one-hundred-fold because every home buyer had a one-hundred-fifty-acre backyard. Buyers enjoyed ducks, birds, squirrels, rabbits, swimming pools, tennis courts, and one-hundred-fifty acres of impeccable golf landscaping and were happy to pay $50,000 per lot. They essentially owned a one-hundred-fifty-and-one-quarter-acre estate, a la a Rockefeller. They had purchased a multi-million dollar backyard on the fairway of a country club for a small amount of club dues. I thought to myself, "Incredible!"

At that time, interestingly enough, Palm Springs was only about a ninety-day season. The second-home or retirement-home market was only 10 percent of the total shelter market. Ninety percent of the marketplace was comprised of primary homes. I recognized that ninety-day season and year-round expenses as distinct disadvantages to the Thunderbird Country Club. But I learned of other places where lots were sold along country club acreage, and by and large, they sold for twice the money per lot and twice as fast as the same lot in the same general market area. The estate-like backyard on the fairway and amenities of golf, tennis, swimming, and the clubhouse made the difference every time. People living on these lots were enjoying an estate-like atmosphere but having to pay a relatively small amount of dues for that enjoyment because other members of the club were paying dues and providing support. And the other people certainly didn't detract from the value. They added to it because you play golf, tennis, and bridge with people. You go to dinner, dancing, and parties with people. They had a place of belonging.

"Pride in belonging" is still very much part of the ClubCorp plan. Perhaps even more so than when we started. America was—and still is—a nation on wheels. People are moving continually and they seek places to belong. They need an extended family, of sorts, when their own family is miles away. I decided to build a Thunderbird-type club in a major metropolitan area, shoot for 90 percent of the market where people lived all year-round, and target the family market with a 365-day season to help the economics of the club. They'd have another reason to buy a home and we'd have a better chance at building a successful club and a better subdivision around it.

In the club business, there's a truism that "As the club goes, so goes the subdivision around it." The reverse is true as well. "As the subdivision goes, so goes the club." Both need to be synergistic and symbiotic with each other because they can make or break one another. I determined that building a flagship club that could successfully stand on its own in a major metropolitan area—as well as bolster the subdivision around it—had to be sensational.

∾

Years ago, I lost count of the number of times that I've been asked why I started ClubCorp. As a rule, depending on the circumstances, I'll usually crack a joke like, "It just seemed like a good idea at the time." Or "I like golf a lot and this gives me the opportunity to play while I work." My motivation, of course, was that my plan was to get rich. It was quite simple. I had spent most of my early years being very, very poor. I wanted to become very, very rich…in business and in life. It's ironic, in a way, that I decided to become a lawyer, so I'd know how to not only make money but also how to keep it. Sometime through the years, the realization hit me. Lawyers, at least at that time, didn't typically become rich by practicing law. Shortly after I began practicing law, someone told me there were only two ways to get rich as a lawyer. One of them was to get out of law school and marry a rich woman, which I hadn't done. The other was to get out of law school, work your tail off for fifty years as a lawyer, and then marry a rich woman. I didn't do that either. But the decisions I made led to 1957 becoming a very good year for me. I founded Country Clubs, Inc. (CCI), the forerunner of the subsidiaries that today make up ClubCorp International. For the record, the charter date for CCI and Brookhaven Country Club in Dallas, Texas, was November 11, 1957. Looking back, setting up Country Clubs, Inc., as the holding company to just do Brookhaven was probably one of the best evidences of practicing the positive attitude that I preach—I was creating a holding company for one club that wasn't even built but obviously had intentions of building more than one.

That year, we also witnessed the birth of my son Bob, who is now chief executive officer and president of ClubCorp. We had been blessed with the arrival of our daughter Patty two years earlier. We could have had more children, but it's like we told Patty and Bob, "Having two such perfect children, we just didn't have any more." Namesake-wise, maybe it's a good thing. A few years ago, my son asked me to move over from being "Bob" to become "Robert," so he could stop being "Bobby" and become "Bob." I assured him I've known some very successful Bobby's, like Bobby Stewart with whom I played tennis at home every week and who was chairman of the largest bank in Texas at the time. Bobby Folsom, another tennis buddy, was a very successful developer and former mayor of Dallas. Bobby Brown from Fort Worth also frequently played tennis with us. He had played on a world championship baseball team and was president of the American Baseball League, as well as a very successful surgeon. My son said, "Look, Dad. Their fathers probably weren't as visible in business circles as you've been. I've never asked you to do very much for me, but I'm asking you to do this." Then he very effectively used one of my own lines against me. He said, "If it's not a big deal to you, it is to me. So just humor me." Calling him Bobby has been a hard habit to break. Trying to be Robert instead of Bob has been difficult, but I'm assiduously making the effort. After all, he's my only son.

∾

Memories of 1957 ebb and flow in my mind. Postage stamps were only three cents. Five thousand dollars would buy a brand new Cadillac. Patti Page was singing "How Much Is That Doggy in the Window?" on the radio, and people were still talking about that shocking beach scene in *From Here to Eternity*. The year marked the fourth year of President Eisenhower's first term. It was the year Orville Faubus stood on the steps of a high school in Little Rock, Arkansas, and said integration would not take place. It was also the year the Russians sent Sputnik I and II to the moon, which helped trigger John Kennedy's intense interest in the space race some years later.

Twelve years had passed since the end of World War II. Many

veterans had returned to the States with their bill of rights to either start college or finish their education. Many already had married the girl next door or their high school sweetheart. The migration to cities from the farm and the small towns that had begun in the 1930s was at an all-time high. Cities were getting bigger. Families were growing. Americans in general were settling into postwar prosperity quite nicely. Buying new homes. Raising children. Driving new cars. Wearing nice clothes. Enjoying their freedoms anew, fresh from the front lines of World War II.

The country club scene of that era was different from what we know today. Clubs that had prospered in the first three decades of this century were sorely tried by the Great Depression, and further brutalized by World War II. More clubs closed than opened in the years between 1930 and 1957. In fact, when Brookhaven swung open its doors in 1958 as our first endeavor, fewer clubs were scattered across the country than in 1930. And the ones that had survived did so with a membership philosophy that revolved around keeping people out, not letting them in. That's not to say there weren't many fine old clubs across the country when ClubCorp was launched, but they essentially served the well-connected and well-to-do.

∾

About the same time I was formulating my club plan, a Dallas real estate developer by the name of Fritz Hawn had purchased the 1,100-acre R.B. George estate, located on the northwestern outskirts of what was then considered Dallas proper. For those of you familiar with the city, there wasn't even an LBJ Freeway (Interstate 635) back then. So this land was on the other side of nowhere, as I like to say, without a home in sight when we signed the deal. This land, just north of Valley View Lane, was really considered out in the country. But I could see it was prime to be developed as a country club development with homes around fingers of golf courses. I persuaded Mr. Hawn to sell me forty acres of land for the clubhouse complex at a bargain price with very little down and a long, slow note. I leased the remainder of the land necessary to build what is now Brookhaven Country Club (for fifty years with an option to purchase). This club—today an institution in its own right—immediately enhanced the value of thousands of surrounding lots.

I then asked myself if there was a way to make Brookhaven more affordable and an even better value so that I could reach further down into the marketing pyramid. The top three clubs in Dallas at the time—the Dallas Country Club, Brook Hollow, and Northwood, in that order—were aimed at the top 1 percent. Their membership focus was primarily on board chairmen, presidents, and people with inherited wealth. They went after the ultra-rich. I decided to devise a club concept that would not only embrace but be affordable to the top 10 percent of the population, including company vice-presidents, doctors, lawyers, accountants, investment bankers, brokers, and airline pilots. I needed to make this club better able to survive by depending upon its own numbers, as opposed to being subsidized by the developer.

My plan has since become a basic primer in club management. It's based on the premise in the golf industry that what money you make on the golf course, you lose in the clubhouse. The principal cost of most country clubs is the clubhouse operations. Golf courses can stand much better on their own, but the clubhouse and ancillary operations can eat their lunch, figuratively speaking. I needed a plan like those two old men in the dungeon. What I came up with was a fifty-four-hole golf concept—build the athletic amenities of three country clubs around one clubhouse. That way, our clubhouse operations would be three times as economically viable as our eighteen-hole competitors. We would have the capital investment in, debt-service on and operating overhead of, only one clubhouse with the athletic amenities and membership of three country clubs. Because of this "three-clubs-in-one" concept, we could afford to pay our pivotal staff members—manager, chef, golf pro, tennis pro, golf course superintendent, and athletic director—one-and-a-half times what the eighteen-hole clubs were paying. This enabled us to get—and keep—the best people in the industry, even though the cost for those superior people was only half as much as the per-member cost to members of other clubs. We had three times the number of members paying those salaries, but not any more crowded conditions on the athletic amenities. That's economy of scale at its very best, and it worked.

Those early days of ClubCorp must have been something like learning to fly a 747 without any experience in aviation. This was about the same time that Elmer Wheeler wrote a book called, *Sell the Sizzle and Not the Steak*. But as I learned from Mr. Hunt, I would take someone else's idea and then add onto it. I'd say, "Sell the sizzle and not the steak, but have a very good steak to sell for a fair price." In the beginning, we were selling the sizzle of belonging to a very fine country club for very affordable initiation fees and membership dues. But we didn't even have the steak yet. The club wasn't even built yet. Selling a concept is really what we had to push in our first year of existence. We did have to have a quality product for a quality price, but then we wanted to sell the sizzle out of it. We were in the sizzle business. We still are. And the plan was working. And still is.

❧

Part of any plan is adjusting to new trends. First, we built country clubs. Then, city clubs. Then, we did consulting for other people about their clubs. Then, we took our club expertise abroad, to Europe and Asia. When the club business started to soften, we began buying resorts. We mainly went into the acquisition business because we could buy country clubs and resorts more economically than we could build them. We kept on founding city clubs, of course, because we were creating an even better industry. But we bought country clubs because we could buy them for about half of what it would cost to build them.

In the early 1960s, I was phasing out my law practice and became the full-time chairman and chief executive officer of the company. The board unanimously approved my initial salary of $12,000 a year, plus expenses, in 1962. Some of our executives joked at the time that this magnificent salary set our compensation pattern for years to come. After country clubs, we debuted the city club concept in 1965. ClubCorp's first city club was the Lancer's in downtown Dallas. When the Lancer's opened, we were like toddlers in the food and beverage world. So we had some real *faux pas* along the way. One of our executives was trying to woo the president of a university who ordered escargot for his wife. She was very excited about trying something new. When the food was served, it came out on a little salad plate with six items that looked like hush puppies. As it turned out, the chef had simply left the snails in their shells, rolled them in some batter and deep fried them. You could hear the "click, click" of the fork against the shell underneath all that batter. Today, it's funny. Back then, we ordered another round of drinks and tried to laugh it off as a learning experience.

∾

I continue to plan the work and work the plan, which means not only growth but succession planning. My son, Bob, became active with the company and served as director of Corporate

Planning from 1980 to 1984. He then went to Salomon Brothers, Inc., where he was an associate specializing in mergers and acquisitions from 1984 to 1987. He came back to us in 1987 as chief financial officer and was elected president in January 1989, overseeing all operational aspects of each ClubCorp subsidiary. In 1998, Bob became chief executive officer. I'm sure I've been both a mentor and a tormentor for him over the years. He's learned from what I did right, and what I did wrong. He's often viewed in my shadow, but we are quite different and together well-matched in management skills. I'm possibly a bit more entrepreneurial, but that's because I had to be and needed to be. I'm more oriented to the need to use other people's money and other people's brains. Those are important, but you have to use them in a winning way. You have to be a good steward, and he's learned that value well. I think he's a bit more organized and definitely more administrative-minded than I am. I never regretted stealing him away from Salomon Brothers, and I'm quite proud of the way he's run things since.

ELEPHANT EARS

When I was in the sixth grade in Rison, I remember a girl who asked me to take her to a particular party or something, and I guess I didn't appear as responsive as she thought I should have been. She huffed, "All right, elephant ears. So much for you." It wasn't until that precise moment—I actually went to a mirror and looked—that I realized she was telling the truth. I did have big ears. Apparently, other people were talking about my ears and I didn't know it. I was twelve years old then and I've been a little self-conscious about the size of my ears ever since.

3

The More You Learn, the More You Earn

As the story goes, Thomas Edison conducted ten thousand experiments before he finally demonstrated the first incandescent light bulb on October 21, 1879. Often ridiculed by his peers, he contended, "I didn't fail ten thousand times. I successfully eliminated, ten thousand times, materials and combinations which wouldn't work." He also said something else that made an impression upon me: "The three great essentials to achieve anything worthwhile are first, hard work; second, stick-to-tiveness; and third, common sense." I believe you need all three attributes in pursuing a college education. After all, there's more to a degree than a piece of paper—that's just a symbol that a young adult embarked on a program, saw it through, and picked up some technical knowledge. It's also a very good insight, a precursor, if you will, to the tenacity and other talents you used in college that will help enhance the rest of your life.

It's possible to be a success without a college education. It's just a lot harder and increasingly more difficult to make and keep a fortune without a college degree. I believe that education begins with listening and leadership starts with learning. It's nice to be smart, but even more important to be educated in many ways. Some people have a quantity of book-learning and almost no common sense. Your natural smarts are polished with a formal education, but don't forget to learn all you can about judgment and practice common sense in the process.

One of the first lessons I learned about business came in the shape of a coat hanger. The tailor in Rison said that he would pay a penny apiece for coat hangers. As a young boy, I didn't waste time. That same day, I went through the house and rounded up all the coat hangers, took them to the tailor, and sold him about a hundred of them, a dollar's worth. When he said he'd buy more, I told other people I'd pay them a half a penny per coat hanger, and then go sell them to the tailor for a penny each. This scenario worked for about a couple hundred coat hangers. Then I hired two other kids to go out and buy coat hangers. To make a long story short, I had flooded the market with coat hangers by about 3 o'clock that afternoon. I ended up with more coat hangers than I could sell, which meant I had to slowly feed them to the tailor over the next two years. I was sitting on inventory that I couldn't liquidate and had used most of the money I had made to build up that surplus inventory. The episode was an invaluable business lesson at a pretty young age about "depth of market" and flooding the market. If I'd been just a little more patient and done only what I could do, I would have made more money. My mistake was trying to be a big shot too quickly, and I paid the price. Experiences like this taught me what I didn't learn in school.

❧

Of all the subjects in school, math in particular came incredibly easy to me. In Rison, I learned how to do square roots from the book. I taught them to the class because the teacher was having the hardest time understanding the concept. And I scored a grade of "100" on every math exam I took for the full four years I spent at North Dallas High School. Some teachers would even put particularly difficult math problems on tests in attempts to stump me, and I'd still make a perfect score. Sometimes they'd have to give me a score of "120," so they could curve the rest of the test scores and other kids could pass the exam.

I excelled, not because I studied a lot, but because I listened in class. I paid attention to the teachers, especially after I figured out that they seldom asked exam questions that hadn't been discussed in class. I had a high degree of comprehension on just about every subject, with the notable exception of chemistry. It was a battle in high school and a full-fledged war in college. To make matters worse, the atomic chart was changing at the time, and the rules of chemistry seemed to be in constant flux. Fortunately, I was good enough in math, English, history, and other subjects to make up for it.

During my school years, I discovered another lesson in education. I learned how to take tests. In history, for example, I'd make sure that I underlined every name and date in my book. That's because just about every event revolved around someone and a date. Teachers would throw in trick questions about people who might not have been significant without a date, but it was almost impossible to score less than "100" if I knew all the people and all the dates listed in that particular time frame. I may not like my "elephant ears," but I've always been very grateful for what's in-between them. I made an "A" for every six weeks' grade, every semester final exam and obviously every semester grade in high school. Without a single "B" for the four years in high school, naturally I was named valedictorian for my North Dallas senior class.

∾

Some of my best school-day lessons came from outside the classroom. In fact, I learned through sports, especially when I was playing baseball in Arkansas before I moved to Dallas. I remember when I came home after the games, my father would ask me how I played. On one particular day, he asked, "How'd you do?" and I said I had four hits. He said, "Now, come on, son. Let's face it. Two of them were fielding errors." Obviously, I'd been found out. "It's always better in life to just tell it like it is," my father said as he left the room. Of course, now I know that there's real power in the spirit of truth. It catches a lot of people off-guard when you just tell the truth—nothing more than what needs to be said and nothing less than what should be said.

I have many memories of those Sunday afternoons during summer, when guys from Rison would play teams from nearby cities like Fordyce, Pine Bluff, Monticello, or Kingsland. Each town would pick its nine best players to make up its home team. Some of these fellows were ex-major leaguers, so going to the game was akin to watching semi-pro baseball. In fact, the games provided one of the main forms of entertainment since we didn't have television sets then. If you were a professional baseball fan, you listened to games on the radio. Sunday afternoon baseball between two Arkansas teams was "real" entertainment you could hear—and see.

Local merchants got into the act by furnishing uniforms for their home teams. In Rison, our sponsor was Turner's Grocery Store. Not only did Mr. Turner supply the uniforms, balls, bats, shoes, and gloves, but he'd also pay us two bits for a single, four bits for a double, six bits for a triple, and a whole dollar for a home run. That was real good money in those days, so he was a real hero. I could throw the ball pretty hard and hit well, too. I was a catcher and sometimes a pitcher, an assignment that made me an even better hitter because a catcher learns to judge the speed and spin of a ball, so it's easier to hit an "in-" or "out-drop." As the ball came off the pitcher's fingers, I could recognize which was which. I'd actually catch a game and pitch a game against some mighty fine competition in double headers on the same day. Barely a teenager, I was playing what amounted to semi-pro baseball.

I'll never forget the first time Rison played the Pine Bluff All-Stars. I was thirteen. The town of Pine Bluff, with a population of about 25,000, was at least twenty-five times the size of Rison. The guys on the other team were so much bigger and older than we were, it was downright intimidating. Well, the visiting team always went to bat first and I remember I was playing outfield at the time. Their first two guys stepped up to the plate and hit home runs! Both of them, on the first or second pitch. As I watched those balls fly over my head and then over the fence, I remember thinking, "Boy, this is going to be the longest day of my life."

The rest of the details are somewhat hazy although I think we eventually got into the game and may have won. But I'll never forget those first two guys as long as I live. I thought, "What if every guy who gets up to bat hits a home run?" And against our best pitcher, too. It was mind-boggling, especially to a kid. I didn't know it at the time, but facing such competition was great preparation for the business world. And it provided preparation to plan for defeats, as well as victories.

～

I made the North Dallas High School varsity baseball team as a freshman, and won a college scholarship after batting what the record books reflected as .563 as a senior. Of course, I could hit and throw harder when I came to high school in Dallas because I was a year older than the other kids. Schools in Texas at that time, by and large, started kids in high school when they were thirteen and ended when they were seventeen. In Arkansas, high school started when kids were fourteen and ended when they were eighteen. I was seventeen, competing against sixteen- and fifteen-year-olds, and eighteen competing against seventeen- and sixteen-year-olds. I always thought I was just superior proto-plasm—in the classroom and in athletics—but I've realized since then that I was better because I was older.

In addition to sports, high school provided many opportunities to discover other talents. Not only was I valedictorian my senior year, I also was editor of the student yearbook and editor of the school newspaper. I was winning trophies in speech almost every weekend and my first scholarship came when I was named the most Outstanding Speaker in the Nation by the Senate of the National Student Congress of the National Forensic League. The Senate of the National Student Congress was comprised of the top boy speaker and top girl speaker from each state, deter-mined by the cumulative number of points won in Debate, Declamation, and Extemporaneous Speaking. The House was comprised of the number of boys and girls equal to the number of representatives from each state, and having the next highest number of points behind the Senators. I was the top boy speaker and boy Senator from Texas because, over four years, I had prob-ably teed it up more than anyone else. I read one time that Mr. Hunt had probably drilled more discovery wells than anyone else. That was probably true because he had also drilled more dry holes than anyone else. These are both good object lessons on the value of persistence and perseverance. The honor wasn't just because of my debating ability. I knew the honor was going to be determined by a vote of all the Senators at the end of the session and I thought I needed the scholarship because I hadn't yet been offered one in baseball. Since the number of male and female senators was identical, I focused on getting the females to vote for me. With my best party manners, I'd take one to breakfast, another to morning coffee, one to lunch, another to dinner, and so on. If she was from Idaho, we'd talk about a potato bill. If she was from Iowa, we'd talk about subsidies to grow corn. If she was from Washington State, we might talk about timber and salmon fishing. By the time the week was over, I'd gotten to know just about every female senator and about her special interests and would help them get their bills passed. I concentrated on getting their votes, not making speeches like almost everyone else. I showed up with a goal—to win their vote—and a plan on how to do it. Everybody else was too busy making speeches to notice my tactics. Obviously, I won overwhelmingly because I had a plan.

∽

I recall other pivotal learning experiences throughout high school. My Latin teacher, Myrtle Clopton, probably had as much motivational influence over my life then as poetry did later, mainly because she thought I was so brilliant. For example, I remember when I was a freshman, she wrote a question in Latin on the blackboard, then asked me to go up and write down the answer in Latin. I did so and sat back down. She asked the class, "Now, what's wrong with what he wrote?" No one answered. Then she said, "I'll tell you what's wrong with it. Nothing." She took a shine to me from that day forward. I later won the state title in Latin, for me…and for her.

By the time I was in the tenth grade, I had memorized Kipling's "If" poem. Sometimes, when I'd be in the middle of a debate tournament or playing tennis or baseball, and be losing, I'd start quoting parts of it silently to myself. If I was dog-tired and felt like giving up, his lines would give me strength. *"If you can force your heart and nerve and sinew to serve your turn long after they are gone./ And so hold on when there is nothing in you except the will which says to them: 'Hold on.'"* In other words, tie a knot at the end of your rope and hang on. Often in life, the words in

Kipling's poem have helped my sometimes tired soul when it came time to get up the next morning and start over. I have probably quoted some part of "If" either out loud or to myself at least every other day since I memorized it in high school. Another line I would repeat a lot in high school was, "If it be Thy will, Lord, please let me win." When I'd be competing, I'd say, "Gee, I'd like to win, but it needs to be Thy will." I believe that I should pray like everything depends upon Him, but work like everything depends upon me. Winning is never easy—and it shouldn't be. I think winning just feels better if I have worked my fanny off.

Toward the end of high school, several baseball scouts expressed interest in signing me up for a pro career, but I had to tell them to forget it, that the Navy owned me. I didn't even get to accept the public speaking scholarship I won or the baseball college scholarships offered after batting that .563 record as a senior. I had joined the Navy, and that was that. I actually signed up before I turned eighteen on February 15, 1944. That way, instead of being drafted, I could finish high school and then report for active duty to the service of my choice.

∾

I reported for duty on June 1, 1944. The Naval Air Corps recruited the elite and I definitely wanted to be part of that elite. The Naval Air Corps was known as the branch of service that required the most cerebral capacity and the best eye/hand coordination. Those who could qualify didn't hesitate to sign up. There seemed to be more navigation to being a pilot in the Naval Air Corps than in the Army Air Corps. Army pilots could follow landmarks like railroad tracks. In the Navy, a pilot would fly off a ship in the middle of the ocean with no tracks to follow, fly for several hours, and then have to make his way back to a ship that had usually been moving the whole time. A Navy pilot had to have a certain amount of mathematical know-how to find his target or his base ship. There were no computers to guide you like there are now. You had to be sharper between the ears to be a Navy pilot.

The downside was that once someone was in this Navy program, there was no acceptable or honorable way to get out until the Navy said, "Go. We don't need you anymore." If you got married, you were kicked out. You could not make your grades or commit some other rules infraction and get busted out. Your health could falter or you could die. I was locked into the program for its duration or until the Navy let me out. The Navy decided I ought to go to college. I didn't have anything to say about the matter, but I sure made the most of it.

∾

When I selected the Navy, I knew I wanted to be a lawyer, but the Naval Air Corps was more interested in turning out fighter pilots than attorneys. But the war was winding down by the time I entered the service. D-Day came, of course, five days later on June 6, and the tide turned in our favor when the Allied Armed Forces invaded Europe. The Navy, in turn, wasn't needing as many pilots by the summer of 1944 as when I signed up earlier that year. So I was sent to North Texas Agricultural College (now The University of Texas at Arlington) instead of the Athens, Georgia, pre-flight school where I was slated to go when I enlisted. I ended up staying at Arlington for one year or three trimesters. Students would go four months for each trimester. You could take more than twenty hours if you made "A's," so I piled up sixty some-odd hours and got my junior college degree in engineering in one year.

That was all I could take there, so the Navy—now in a

holding pattern—sent me to Texas Christian University in Fort Worth for a semester. I think the original program was called V-5, which participants laughingly claimed stood for "Victory in Five Years or We Fight." The program was known as V-12 Aviation by the time I went to TCU. At the end of that semester, the Navy still wanted to keep me, so I was sent to The University of Texas at Austin to be part of an extension of the Navy's officers program at Annapolis, known as the Naval Reserve Officers Training Corps (NROTC).

All this time I was putting in eighty-hour weeks by having two full-time jobs. One was going to school. The other was playing sailor. That's why I took so many extra hours in Arlington to get my junior college degree, did two years worth of work in one year there, and took extra elective hours in economics to get a combination economics and law degree while I was at The University of Texas. It seems impossible that I could get three full degrees in four years, while spending two years in the Navy full-time, getting an Ensign's commission, and working full-time selling insurance and real estate the last two years while getting my economics and law degrees. I'd only been out of high school for four years, but that's what happened. I finally entered law school in 1946 when I graduated from The University of Texas at Austin. The Navy was releasing men from active duty by that time and I went into the Naval Reserve Officer Corps because the war was over. I remained a reserve officer for two more years until I reached the level of Lieutenant J-G. Then the Navy kicked me out for good.

Again, planning and time-management were important facets of my life. I went to law school fourteen hours a week, sold insurance during the week and real estate on the weekends, and treated my law classes like appointments. Although the only grade you made in law school was the final exam, you had to show up for classes or you couldn't take the final exam. I studied for the exam on the weekends while I sat on houses and tried to sell them. Thus, I was able to get my law degree, work full-time, and make good money. Looking back, I may have pushed so hard in college because I knew that options such as being a pro-baseball player or taking advantage of college scholarships vanished when the war came along. I had to go into the service and the Navy ruled my life for as long as it saw fit. Like so many others, I sometimes felt like a puppet on a string during the war, but I worked hard to take control of my life again when the cord was cut. Perhaps I pushed so hard to make up for what I felt was lost time. I really don't know.

∽

Along the way, I became absolutely convinced that the more you learn, the more you earn, but more importantly, the more you learn, the more you live. You don't have to know about music or understand art or distinguish fine wines to enjoy them, but the more you know about them, the more you can enjoy them. And the more you enjoy life, the more you live it. When our kids were growing up, Nancy and I made this point using an analogy that started with a rock. We'd say, "This rock doesn't live. It's inanimate. It just sits there. It doesn't know hot or cold, wet or dry, anything at all. Plants, on the other hand, have a much higher capacity for living. Plants know hot and cold, wet and dry, and maybe even respond when you talk to them. Puppies definitely respond to others around them. They live more intently, too, because they have a brain. They know anger, fear, hunger, love, and hate. They have an even higher capacity for living and give unconditional love to almost anyone. They can even learn that if they do certain tricks, they will be rewarded. But God gave man an infinite capacity for living because He gave us a brain to comprehend and enjoy everything that exists in the universe. So

61

the more you expand your breadth of knowledge, the more you live."

I wish I had taken more horticulture in school because I'd like to know more about trees. Emerson said that "beauty is its own excuse for being." I see trees as living sculptures by God and constant earthly reminders of His continuing love for mankind. I don't just see trunks and branches. I see a sculpture. The live oak trees that are plentiful in Texas are incredible sculptures because each is so different. Likewise, it's nice to observe and be interested in architecture without feeling like you have to become an architect. Out of the great Chicago fire, the Chicago School of Architecture was born. Products of that school include Frank Lloyd Wright, known for his angles and overly-complicated twists and turns, and Mies van der Rohe, recognized for his "less is more" approach. Wright once said, "The physician can bury his mistakes, but the architect can only advise his client to plant vines." What a magnificent city Chicago has become, much like a beautiful phoenix rising from the ashes. To me, it's fun to learn about famous architects and the shapes and forms that made them notable—and what they were trying to capture in the essence of their buildings. Then instead of just seeing steel walls and colored glass on the horizon, you see something more. You experience it and you live it.

There's an Irish toast that goes something like this: "May you really live as long as you live." In other words, may you really live all of your life. We should all strive to add life to our years, not just years to our lives. When you add life to your years and years to your life, you really get the most enjoyment of the life you live.

Nancy epitomizes the thrill of lifetime learning more than anyone else I know. She started by being a Phi Beta Kappa in college and has constantly honed her language skills in Spanish, French, and Italian. She has constantly aspired to learn about cuisine and wine. She has studied with nearly all of the top master chefs in Europe and wrote two cookbooks that are very much appreciated by her friends and our chefs. She also works at learning more about art, antiques, and architecture. She's no stranger to fashion either, evidenced by her being elected as one of the ten best-dressed women in Dallas three times. She finally was retired to the Fashion Hall of Fame so that she would no longer be perceived as competing with the other women vying for the best-dressed list. Nancy is a lifetime learner, probably the most cultured person I know and a tremendous help in growing ClubCorp.

❧

Eleanor Roosevelt once said, "You must do the thing you think you cannot do. Life was meant to be lived and curiosity must be kept alive. One must never, for whatever reason, turn his back on life." Expanding your knowledge and bettering your life are the primary reasons for colleges and universities to exist, in my opinion. A university is a college of arts and sciences, surrounded by trade schools in specialty areas like law, business, engineering, medicine, etc. Students should learn as much as they can about psychology, English, history, literature, and foreign language, etc., before, during, and after their individual professions. The more they learn about each of these disciplines, the better they'll be able to perform in their chosen profession. Physics and mathematics help teach the discipline of precise thinking. These subjects also are tremendously helpful in professional endeavors. My advice is that the more you learn about all of them, the better you'll do in business, but even more important, the richer your life will be.

The same holds true for words. I've read that word power is the single most common denominator among super-achievers. Their command of the English language and their ability to work its dynamics set them apart. Nearly all decisions of any magnitude are group decisions. So whoever has the best idea and is able to express it the best, naturally floats to the top. To paraphrase the Bible, when you have a good idea, but can't express it, it's like having "a light underneath a basket." No one knows it's there. But even more important, the ability to have a good idea is either enhanced or inhibited by word power. People think in words. You can't think what you don't know how to say. Your brain comes up with ideas based on concepts and conclusions that are as strong, or weak, as your vocabulary.

Here's an example. Let's say you know that the term *synergy* describes a situation where the total exceeds the sum of the parts. When you add one plus one, you get three. We use this concept in ClubCorp in the resort business. Here's how: The rooms should make money (let's say a dollar). The homes and the land development around them should make money (let's say another dollar). Add them together synergistically and we should get four dollars, not just two. In addition, recreational amenities should make money (again, let's say one dollar). When you add them together, they are so synergistic and symbiotic with each other that their total value adds up to six dollars, not just three.

The term *symbiotic* means interdependent and mutually supporting. In Texas, you know if you plant a pound of bluebonnet seeds and a pound of Indian paintbrush seeds, you'll get three pounds of effect. Each grows and blooms because of the synergistic, symbiotic relationship between bluebonnets and Indian paintbrushes. If you understand how to use both of these concepts, your idea can be the one that floats to the top. You conjure up the same kind of winning conclusions by explaining, "We need to set up a synergistic, symbiotic relationship." Everybody wins. Everybody listens. It's very difficult to come up with the concept if you don't know the words, and even more difficult, to sell it. Your ability to "enroll" others can often make or break a good idea.

❧

There's just no substitute for smarts. I'll use a joke to prove my point. This fellow has a flat tire, so he pulls over to the side of the road and starts to change it. He takes all the lugs off the right rear wheel and puts them into the hubcap. A gust of wind comes along and overturns the hubcap. The lugs fall into a nearby stream and are swept away. The fellow's up a creek now. He hadn't noticed that just on the other side of the stream is an insane asylum. One of the inmates inside the fence had been watching him the whole time. The inmate hollered at the guy, "Why don't you take one lug off each of the other three wheels and put them on the right rear wheel? I'm sure you could make it to the next town that way." The guy with the flat tire is impressed with the idea and says, "Hey, that's a good one. If you're so smart, why are you in an insane asylum?" The fellow behind the fence says, "Mister, we're in here because we're crazy, not stupid."

Always move ahead. Don't be a re-run. A joke I tell to make this point in speeches is about a couple of drunks who are sitting in a bar and watching the 10 o'clock news. This guy is out on the ledge of a building and he's obviously thinking about jumping. The fire trucks are there. Search lights. Police. The press. One of these drunks says to the other, "I'll bet you $100 that he jumps." The second one says, "Okay, I'll take that bet." Well, sure enough, the fellow jumps. The second guy pulls out his wallet to pay off the first one, and the first one says, "You know, I can't take your money. I saw this on the 8 o'clock news and I knew he'd jump." The second guy says, "That's all right. Go ahead and take it. I saw the 8 o'clock news, too. I just didn't think the damn fool would do it again."

Something else Eleanor Roosevelt once said was, "You learn by living. When you cease to make a contribution, you begin to die." Make it a goal to learn something new every day of your life that either will enhance your earning power, your enjoyment of living, or both. It really doesn't matter what or how much you know now. It's more important to learn all you can for as long as you can. Different languages. Different cultures. Exciting concepts. Listen a lot. Stay informed. Never stop reading. Cherish your excitement over each new word, fact, thought, talent, or idea you learn. As long as you're learning, your brain keeps growing. Your body may be aging but your ability to stay young depends upon your mind's capacity for continuous learning. Your mind has the ability to stay alive for as long as you learn.

Great Minds Think Alike

I believe great minds think alike. Here's what I mean:

"Wealth is not his that has it, but his that enjoys it."
— Benjamin Franklin

"Paying attention to simple little things that most men neglect makes a few men rich."
— Henry Ford

"As a man thinketh so is he, and as a man chooseth so is he."
— Ralph Waldo Emerson

"Try not to become a man of success but rather try to become a man of value."
— Albert Einstein

"It is an unfortunate human failing that a full pocketbook often groans more loudly than an empty stomach."
— Franklin D. Roosevelt

"The sole purpose of being rich is to give away money."
— Andrew Carnegie

"Put the customer first, communicate, keep your ear to the ground, push responsibility and authority down, force ideas to bubble up, stay lean and fight bureaucracy, and always give something back."
— Sam Walton

"The Lord prefers common-looking people. That is why he made so many of them."
—Abraham Lincoln

"Every problem has in it the seeds of its own solution. If you don't have any problems, you don't get any seeds."
— Dr. Norman Vincent Peale

"Dream as though you'll live forever. Live as if you'll die today."
—James Dean

POSITIVE THINKING

When I was growing up in Arkansas, I would on occasion chase the geese out of the garden in our backyard. On this particular day, though, I was having a lot of trouble catching just one. This fellow walked up and asked me, "Son, how many have you caught so far?" My reply was, "As soon as I catch the one I'm after and four more, I'll have five."

I think of that story often. Another one I like quite a bit is this: Two frogs fall into a gallon of milk. One gives up quickly and drowns. The other has such a positive mental attitude (and the "never-give-up" attitude that goes with it) that he keeps swimming until the milk turns to clabber, then the clabber turns to buttermilk with butter on top. The positive frog walks to safety across the layer of butter.

4

If You Don't Have a Positive Mental Attitude, Get One

If there's one thing that you could give your children that's more important than anything money can buy, it's a positive mental attitude. Children may be born with certain genetic characteristics, but their attitudes and behaviors are developed over time. Children learn and mimic what they see and hear every day—sometimes to their own detriment. That's why it's the parents' responsibility to make sure daily surroundings are as positive as they want their children to be. A parent's positive mental attitude can really make a difference. It gives children, even as youngsters, the will to be happy and the desire to succeed. They learn to be victors, not victims. They seek ways to turn lemons into lemonade and adversity into advantage, and to possess the strength to endure even when they cannot turn the tide. What's more, they'll never be alone. Others will enjoy being around them because they're typically upbeat and would rather be happy than sad. The more fun they are, the more fun they have. The more fun they share with others, the longer and happier lives they will live.

My mother thought I was sensational. So much so, I credit her for the seeds of the positive mental attitude I have maintained throughout life. She used to tell me that everything about me was great. Lips, face, eyes, eye-lashes, smile, fingers, fingernails—like I said, everything. My mother seemed to be so captivated, even mesmerized by me, that she thought I was smart even when I was being a brat. I'd tell her, "Okay, since you don't love me, I'm just going to go into the woods and let the bears eat me up." She later told me how difficult it was to remain angry in the face of such clever play-acting. In fact, she probably overdid the flattery, but I guess most mothers do indulge their children.

Then there was Aunt Virge—Virginia Dedman Blaine was her real name—another significant influence on my positive mental attitude while I lived with her and went to high school in Dallas. She was continually coaching me, although most of the time, I didn't even know it. She probably gave me much of what could be called my diploma in life, or the "thesaurus" of my brain. What a magnificent gift! And, as you already know, a few great poets and their enduring words inspired me to acquire and keep a positive mental attitude. Their poems gave me the power of positive thinking long before the concept was popular and the topic of many self-help books. I had a positive mental attitude before books like *The Power of Positive Thinking* or *I'm Okay, You're Okay* or *Think and Grow Rich* were ever written. By the way, I've read them all and these are super books, but the last one should have been, *Think and Grow Rich In More Than Money*. The book delivers a very positive message about the fact that you can get what you want if you give other people what they want. In other words, you'll be a success in direct proportion to how well you build other people and institutions. All of these are positive messages and well worth repeating, but for me, the ideas first came from my family and poetry.

ॐ

At ClubCorp, we developed a philosophy of hiring attitude over aptitude. That may sound somewhat strange, but the approach has proven to be quite savvy. We believe someone's *attitude*—even more than their *aptitude*—ultimately will determine the *altitude* that they're able to reach within the company—and in life. Nowadays, too many people want to get rich at the expense of someone else. Too many people would rather skip through life—not as victors, but as victims. They'd rather quit than lose. They prefer to fail than fight. I don't understand it. I'm not much on failure for the same reason that a disillusioned Norman Schwarzkopf, who led the U.S. triumph in the Persian Gulf War, said he stayed in the military after the Vietnam War. He realized that you are not defeated when you lose. You're only defeated when you quit.

Did you know that Michael Jordan, who today graces the hoops as one of the greatest basketball players of all time, was cut from his high school basketball team? He once was quoted: "Obstacles don't have to stop you. If you run into a wall, don't turn around and give up. Figure out how to climb it, go through it, or work around it." Or that Sandra Day O'Connor was offered only one job out of law school—as a legal secretary? Some years later, she became the first woman ever to sit on the United States Supreme Court. Attitude is more than a state of mind. It translates into behavior. What's more, we are all managers of our own behavior. One of my favorite mottoes is a Latin expression, *carpe diem*, which means, "Seize the Day." In other words, go for it. Live a lot. Live out loud. Have a joy of living. People will notice. They may not be able to pinpoint precisely what makes you different, just that you are.

ॐ

That's not to say that even positive people sometimes don't get down. Maybe it sounds corny (or at least like an old song), but whenever I do, I start counting my blessings. It usually doesn't take long for me to realize how many I have and my spirits rise rather quickly. Something I've noticed over the years is that my vulnerability increases when my resistance decreases. The times when I'm extra tired are often when my attitude suffers the most. Just a simple good night's sleep is one of the best ways to get recharged. Like Shakespeare's Macbeth says, "Sleep that knits up the ravell'd sleeve of care,/ The death of each day's life, sore labour's bath,/ Balm of hurt minds, great nature's second course." If you get plenty of sleep, your chances greatly increase of waking up refreshed and recharged every day.

Our two-year-old grandson might be the most charming example that I've ever seen of an incredibly positive mental attitude that seems to recharge itself every day. Jeffrey is pint-size, but his words carried a mighty punch one Saturday. He was making an all-out effort to join his older brother and sister for an overnight trip to our house. We had not planned to include Jeffrey because he wasn't quite old enough to go to church with us Sunday morning. We had Jonathan and Christina's overnight bags ready when Jeffrey decided to pull out all the stops. As his eyes filled with big tears that he wouldn't let drop, he smiled and said, "You can take me, too. I no trouble. I wake up happy." The next time we had Jonathan and Christina over to spend the night at our house, we had Jeffrey, too. And sure enough, when he woke up the next morning, he announced for everyone to hear, "I'm happy!"

Little Jeffrey didn't acquire this attitude all by himself. He has somebody who makes him feel super all the time—his mother, our daughter, Patty. She's always so "up" and keeps her attitude about life so positive, that people often call her "Positive Patty." She was given her nickname because everybody remembers her laughing a lot and being such a delightful, positive person to be around. Patty's been a sheer joy—like a fresh breath of spring—ever since she was born. She enjoys life and loves being a feminine female. You can't be with her without smiling and laughing and feeling good. She makes a very positive contribution to her family, her children, to our company, and to others.

Patty also has a passion about life that won't allow her to go through the motions. She never does anything halfway. She's always right in the middle of whatever. Her joy of living is unsinkable.

❧

At ClubCorp, we have programs in place to encourage our employee partners to think and act with positive mental attitudes in their dealings with colleagues and members alike. The programs start with everybody's two favorite words: The sound of his or her own name. We address our members by name every chance we get. After all, people join private clubs because they want to feel special. Everything we do is done with that goal in mind. We treat our members like kings and queens. The resorts abide by the slogan "Where Every Guest Is A Member." Our goal is to make guests feel special in every way all the time. Our Number One rule is: "Our members are always right." Our Number Two rule is: "Anytime members may appear to be wrong, remember the Number One rule."

We use high tech to do a better job of delivering high touch and consistently living up to our members' expectations. To us, high tech is more than crunching the numbers. We try to anticipate their desires. We maintain computer set-ups on each of our member partners—age, spouse, likes, dislikes, what they drink, where they like to sit, even whether they prefer margarine over butter. We want to surprise them with what they want before they have to tell us more than once. The late President John F. Kennedy said, "Man is still the most extraordinary computer of all." I would agree, but in this age of high technology, we haven't fallen behind in the computer department.

Our positive attitude stretches from the board room to the dining room throughout ClubCorp properties. It directs us in the selection and development of professionals who are experienced in the private club business. We employ landscape architects and college-degreed agronomists to maintain our golf courses to superior quality standards. We use professionals trained in specific areas, such as food and beverage, catering, and membership development. We provide our employee partners with in-depth, on-going training at every level. We encourage aspiring club mangers to undergo extensive training on subjects ranging from wine regions to labor law to the finer points of dining etiquette. The success of our training programs is measured continuously. We test our people on a variety of subjects, and there's a formal—and often unannounced—inspection of every club at least once a year. In keeping with our priorities, though, the ultimate evaluators are our members. We have a set of quality standards, but club managers are encouraged to make decisions for themselves and go beyond those standards depending on the needs of the club's membership. We hire independent research firms to perform annual, in-depth surveys of every club's membership and staff, and compare the results to a substantial database. Our managers are compensated on performance and receive bonuses for any enhancements. Bonuses are based on achieving quantitative scores such as financial goals, but they are also influenced by qualitative ratings like member surveys, inspection scores, and employee attitude surveys. We use the surveys and research to improve operations and we especially try to make the members feel that their opinions count. In each issue of *Private Clubs* magazine, there is a brief story about an improvement at a club that resulted from a suggestion in a member survey. We call the feature, "You Make A Difference."

∽

I credit another degree of my success to the management approach of surrounding myself with people I consider smarter than me. I often say that the more our people do and the less I do, the better we do. There are many smart people in the world who love to work with and for somebody who genuinely appreciates them. That was one of the greatest talents of my friend Sam Walton, founder of Wal-Mart. He truly appreciated people and he never hesitated to tell them just that. Whenever I went to a Wal-Mart board meeting, he would thank me for being on the board and coming to the meetings. He was so solicitous of my opinion on so many subjects that I genuinely enjoyed being around him because he made me feel that I was making an important contribution. Just being around him was a real thrill because he was such a humble, talented, considerate person. He always tried to make other people feel good.

No matter how large ClubCorp becomes, we operate better when the attitude is that of a "we" company, not an "I" company. "I-itis" is one of the worst diseases an executive can have. One of the best things a good manager can learn is the importance of the word, "we," and the self-limitations of the word, "I." It's one of the littlest words in the human vocabulary, and people who use it excessively are usually equally as little in the eyes of others. The quicker a manager learns how to use the big "we," the better off he or she will be.

Building relationships with a "win-win" attitude is the key to success, in business and in life. A lot of people think it takes a dog-eat-dog attitude to succeed. They think success only comes at the expense of someone else. To win, someone has to lose. This may be true in sports and in cards where there are winners and losers, but not in life. When one person is winning at the expense of another, the loser usually terminates the relationship, and then both become losers. There is no winner. That's why the enduring success of personal and business relationships is the ultimate measure of success in life.

The Pony Story

When I am having trouble finding the right synergy between us and a potential deal, I'll pull out my pony story. It's all about attitude, and goes like this: A couple has twins. One is an extreme optimist and the other an extreme pessimist. These two kids have vastly divergent personalities. Little Happy Johnny can't be fazed by anything and Little Sad Sam can't be pleased by anything. The parents decide to consult a psychiatrist on what to do. They explain the problem and the doctor suggests they try what might be loosely described as reverse psychology on them. He tells them, "Christmas is coming up, so give Little Sad Sam everything he could possibly want and Little Happy Johnny nothing, and maybe that will shock them out of their extreme personalities." Christmas morning comes. Little Sad Sam has everything a little boy could conceivably want under the tree, while Little Happy Johnny got a bag of horse manure. The father says, "Sam, what did you get?" Little Sad Sam says, "Well, I got a bike, but I'll probably fall off and break my leg. I got a ball, but if I throw it, I have to go get it before I can throw it again. I got some skates, but they'll probably roll out from under me and I'll break my back." And so it went with everything Little Sad Sam got. Little Happy Johnny, meanwhile, is holding his bag of manure and running all over the house, up and down the stairs, opening and closing all the doors, going out into the yard, up to the attic, and down to the basement. When his father asks Johnny, "What did you get?", he says, "Well, Dad, I'm sure I got a pony. I'm just having a hard time finding it." That's what I tell the other party while negotiating a deal. I'm sure there is a pony here. And we ought to be able to find it. We're just having a hard time doing it.

MAKE 'EM LAUGH...

True Texans take a real fancy to this joke, especially if it's told with a Texas-size accent. Do you know the difference between a fairy tale and a Texas tale? A fairy tale commences, "Once upon a time," and a Texas tale begins with, "Now, you sum bitches ain't gonna believe this."

5

Humor Helps

L aughter isn't just good for your soul. It may benefit your body as well. Studies have shown that laughter boosts your immune system and keeps it humming for a full day or more. In a sense, laughter is like any other habit. The more you do it, the more natural it becomes. I once read a super quote from Oscar award-winning actress Emma Thompson, whose childhood was rough after the premature death of her father. She said, "My parents always lightened the mood. In the face of real difficulties, disability, and death, they coped with wit and a sense of fun. For them, the important thing was to laugh—even when they felt like crying." Now that she's reached middle age, she said, "I've come to enjoy the apparent contradictions in myself, since I'm old enough to have a sense of humor about them. Isn't that what growing up is all about—accepting who you are?"

When I was a single, young lawyer, I had a maid who was a brilliant woman with a marvelous sense of humor. I was already twenty-six and not married, and in those days, that was perceived as being old for a bachelor. Almost every week, she'd ask me if I realized I was getting "more particular and less desirable" all the time. We'd always share a laugh over that because her repetition caused me to consider marriage hard, instead of hardly at all. Quite frankly, I'd assumed marriage would happen much later. My attitude was similar to a joke that I heard the other day. This ninety-year-old man is having a physical examination, and his doctor asks, "How old was your father when he died?" The man says, "Did I say he was dead? He's actually one-hundred-twenty years old and getting married for the sixth time." The doctor can't believe his ears. He asks, "Why in the world would a one-hundred-twenty-year-old man want to get married?" The man says, "Who said he wanted to get married?" Someone once asked Katherine Hepburn why she had never married. She said, "Why should I exchange the compliments of many for the constant criticism of one?"

My maid also had some very profound observations about life. Although she was not well-schooled, she was one of the most naturally smart people I've ever met. Some of her truisms included: "If you don't know you're living, you ain't" and "If you're lucky and know you're lucky, you're doubly lucky." She had tremendous wisdom and she treated the negative things that happened to her in a refreshingly funny way. Some aspects of her life may have been hard, but her attitude was always positive. She also used to say, "I have an unshakable conviction that right will win and wrong will lay down and die." I said this to my grandson Jonathan the other day after he almost whipped me in tennis. He won the first two games overwhelmingly, but he became flustered for any number of reasons. I had a new racquet that I was getting to know, so the longer I played, the better my shots. Although I was losing, I still had an unshakable conviction that I would ultimately prevail. I did beat him but the game went beyond winning and losing. On our drive home, I shared with him what my maid used to say to help illustrate this valuable lesson in life.

∞

A mutual sense of humor is one of the reasons that Nancy and I have gotten along so well through all these years. We don't take ourselves too seriously. Upon occasion, I'll poke fun at her when people say, "How's your wife?" I'll say, "Oh, she's very even-tempered. She stays mad all the time." Most will quip, "If I were married to you, I can understand why." She has her moments, too. People tell her that she's so positive and then ask, "Do you ever wake up grumpy?" She says, "Oh, sure, but usually I just let him sleep." Those are some of the ways we tease each other a little bit. We believe in that old Scottish saying that angels can fly because they take themselves lightly.

It's important in life to take your assignments seriously and your problems seriously, but never yourself too seriously. Because if you do, you can become so tense and intense that you can lose your sense of humor. When that happens, you lose your ability to see problems in perspective. You also lose the positive mental attitude that it takes to seek and find solutions to those problems. Gone are the persuasive skills required to build the consensus necessary to solve the big problems. Gone are the leadership skills required to implement the solutions with people. Nobody likes to follow a sourpuss. Everybody likes to be with somebody who seeks solutions and has a positive attitude toward finding and implementing them.

There's a lot more to humor than what it can do to you. It's also important what humor can do for you. It was indeed a merciful God who invented laughter; because the more we laugh, the more we live. And there's a beautiful message in laughter itself. As a rule, to have laughter, we have to give it to someone else. When we give laughter, the more we have ourselves. The more you give laughter to someone else, obviously, the more you enjoy it yourself. Just as obvious to me, there's another beautiful message here—the more you give, the more you live.

∾

Some people refer to me as a jokester because I tell a lot of jokes. It's true, I love to laugh. And I love to make other people laugh. I also know first-hand about humor's tremendous power to turn adversity into advantage. Laughter and the positive mental attitude it cultivates helped me "rescue" my grandson Jonathan at a crucial time in his childhood. Jonathan had always been nurtured, perhaps overly so, by attentive parents. As a first child, he naturally was spoiled. He also had four doting grandparents who thought he could do no wrong. If anything, he was being overly endowed with a positive self-image. Then the bottom fell out. His adorable baby sister Christina was born. To Jonathan's thinking, he went from sensational to chopped liver overnight. Suddenly, all he ever heard was "Jonathan, don't wake up Christina." "Jonathan, don't bother your little sister." And he heard that from all of us, not just his parents. The attention that had once been his now belonged to a little pink, squirming bundle of joy named Christina.

For about two years, I watched my grandson become increasingly down in the dumps. His personality was changing and not for the better. He actually began walking with his shoulders slumped over. When he said or did something wrong and was corrected, he began responding, "Well, what did you expect? I just can't do anything right." I began feeling as if he might need psychiatric help, but before recommending anything so drastic, I decided that I would try to help him get his positive attitude back. I enlisted the aid of humor. I started teaching him jokes that he could tell other people and make them laugh. When they did laugh, he felt important. My plan worked. He even got to the point where he started his talks at school with a joke and was making A-pluses. What's more important, others perceived him as a happy guy who was their pal. To this day, almost every time we get together, he asks, "Granddaddy, do you have another joke for me?" If I do, I tell him and we share a little joy. If not, he usually tells me a joke or two. He's in his teens now, but I'll never forget his transformation to a funny friend who still laughs a lot, tells jokes, and makes other people laugh. Including me.

One time, when Jonathan was on the young side, we were playing golf. He discovered that he didn't have his putter on the first green. Looking in his bag, he didn't have his 9-iron or his 6-iron either. I asked him what had happened to his sticks, and he said, "Well, Granddaddy, I guess I lost them yesterday, playing with my dad." I told him, "Jonathan, I can see losing three golf balls in one round, but I've never seen anyone lose three golf sticks. How can that be?"

You know what he said? "Well, Granddaddy, I guess I just had a bad day." That made me laugh out loud. Humor put a different perspective on the whole thing. The "down-in-the-dumps" Jonathan would have thought he was a bad boy who couldn't do anything right. The "new" Jonathan took it in stride. Losing three golf sticks in one day is a bad deal for any golfer, but humor helped Jonathan turn a lemon into lemonade. And he's never lost that ability since. Interestingly enough, Jonathan found his sticks the next day in the pro shop at Gleneagles Country Club. I tell the story to make the point that the effects of humor don't just create the facade of a positive mental attitude. Telling a lot of jokes and seeing the humor in life's situations really cement an unsinkable positive mental attitude.

Christina, too, has provided laughter for the family. One Easter weekend, Nancy and I took our three grandchildren to Barton Creek in Austin, minus their parents who had gone to Mexico together. We were sitting around, thinking the children were absorbed in their own activities. The oldest, Jonathan, was watching a television movie. Christina and the youngest, Jeffrey, were quietly playing with their Easter baskets. That's what we thought anyway. Nancy and I were discussing a study that she'd recently read about first-born children being super-achievers. The study reported that first-borns are generally the most successful in their life's accomplishments. At that precise moment,

Christina looked up and said, "Well, that's not going to happen in this family." Nancy and I thought she said it with such surprising conviction for a seven-year-old. What's even more amazing is that she just might be right—she's such a little competitor already.

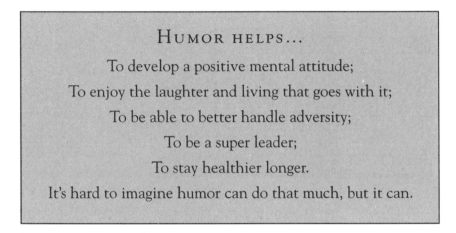

HUMOR HELPS...

To develop a positive mental attitude;

To enjoy the laughter and living that goes with it;

To be able to better handle adversity;

To be a super leader;

To stay healthier longer.

It's hard to imagine humor can do that much, but it can.

Business also has its share of humor. Have you heard the developer's creed? "A dollar borrowed is a dollar earned. A dollar refinanced is a dollar saved. A dollar paid back is a dollar lost forever." Or the CEO's creed? "Debt that does not come due before I retire or sell my stock is equity." Or the banker's creed? "A rolling loan gathers no loss." Or the syndicator's creed? "When you start a syndication, the syndicators have all the knowledge and experience, and the investors all the money. Three years later, the syndicators have all the money and the investors a lot more knowledge and experience."

I've used humor many times over the years in negotiating deals for ClubCorp. Such stories can effectively make a salient point behind the mask of humor. One such story has been particularly effective for me in dealing with developers who may have been successful in some projects, but need to do something with a country club that is losing money. I'll say, "For a developer to get rid of a country club after he's developed the land around it is like making love to a female gorilla. You're not through until she's through." It's been difficult to explain to some visitors why I have a whole shelf of monkeys in my office! But they've been sent to me over the years by developers who said that one joke clinched their decision to do the deal.

My recall for nearly all the stories I know is usually triggered when somebody else paints a picture for me. I see the joke when somebody else paints the picture that *is* the joke. I've told this story when people are trying to sell us a golf course or an operation that's losing money. I'll say this all reminds me a little bit about the chicken and the pig. The chicken says to the pig, "You and I are peculiarly suited to go into business together. We could set up a ham and egger. I'll furnish the eggs, and you'll furnish the ham." The pig thinks for a minute or two, and says, "That's all well and good for you, but I'm afraid it would cost me my ass." Or sometimes, I'll say, "We need to do this deal like porcupines make love. Very carefully."

I also remember some tense negotiations, during which we had been trading a long time and the other side just kept asking for more. To turn the tide, I'd tell the story about how oculists are taught to price eyeglasses. They're instructed to put the glasses on the patient and when he or she says, "How much?" the doctor is supposed to say, "Well, that'll be $200." And if the patient doesn't flinch visibly, the doctor is supposed to continue and add, "for the frames, and $100 for the lenses." And if the patient still hasn't flinched visibly, the doctor is supposed to say, "Each." I've told that story on several occasions when someone had just traded past the point of diminishing returns. I'd say, "Now I want you to know, I'm flinching visibly. This deal is all right for you, but it's getting a little tough for us."

Even sick humor helps. You've probably heard someone say, "It always gets darkest just before it goes completely black." Or, "Cheer up, things could be worse. So I cheered up and sure enough, things got worse." Or, "There's a light at the end of every tunnel. I was elated when I thought I saw one, but dejected when I realized it was a train." One of my favorite parables is this version of Murphy's Law: "If anything can go wrong, it will. Nothing is as simple as it seems. Everything takes longer than you think it will. And if you drop a piece of toast with butter and jelly on it and it falls to the floor, the probability of it landing jelly side down is directly proportional to the price of the carpet."

It helped to have a sense of humor when ClubCorp met hard times head-on. We were growing by 30 percent a year until the early 1980s, when the complexion of the company changed forever. Like many other industries, we were negatively impacted by our nation's down-spiraling economy. We were not immune to the general meltdown. Real estate values collapsed. Banks failed and consolidated in Texas. Oil prices fell below $12 a barrel. The rig count in Texas alone dropped from 4,600 to 600. Buildings that housed our city clubs were vacant. Central business districts in many markets went backward. Five million white-collar executives lost their jobs during this turmoil and consolidation. And most of them were what we call "club-able."

We made a mistake by concentrating so much of our business in the Southwest. Our club division was hit hard by the oil business decline. Hard times also took a toll on our company's morale. There were days when it wasn't much fun to come to work. But these were the kinds of times that build character. And humor became an essential ingredient in our business strategy. I often told the story of a father who had a military approach to bringing up his three sons. He had a ten-year-old, an eight-year-old, and a six-year-old. He'd line them up every morning for inspection and say, "Front and center." The oldest would jump forward and the father would examine his shoes to see if they were polished, and his fingernails to see if they were clean, and then he'd check his appearance to see if he had brushed his teeth and combed his hair. The father would say, "Any questions?" The oldest replied, "No, sir," and the father said, "As you were." He'd go through the same litany with the eight-year-old, and finally got to the six-year-old. He said, "Front and center." The third son stood there as his father berated him for his shoes and his hands being dirty and then asked, "Any questions?" The little kid said, "Yes, sir. How do you get a transfer out of this crummy outfit?" I'm sure there were days back then that some of our key people just wanted a transfer if there were somewhere else to go. Luckily, we all had a sense of humor during the tough times and got through it together.

ॐ

Everybody faces adversity. It brings out the strengths in people, and the good ones rise above it. Like these four men who went on a hunting trip together, one of them a notorious snorer. The other three drew straws to see which one had to sleep in the same room with the snorer. The fellow with the shortest straw spent the night with the snorer, but looked well-rested the next morning. The other guys asked, "How'd you sleep?" And he said, "Fine. When my roommate started snoring, I went over and kissed him on the mouth. I didn't hear another peep out of him all night long."

Some of My Favorites

Like any jokester, I have a few favorites. Some of them are even printable:

A mother goes to wake up her son so he can get ready for church. She tells him it's time to get ready for church on Sunday morning, and he says, "Mother, I'm not going to church this morning for three reasons. First, I'm tired. Second, they don't like me, and third, I don't like them." His mother stomps her foot and says, "Son, you are going to church for two reasons. First, you're forty-six years old, and have always gone to church, and second, you're the pastor."

∾

This couple have been married for fifty years, and both are getting a little hard of hearing. The fellow reaches over and pats his partner on the leg, saying, "Honey, I'm proud of you." She turns to look at him and says, "Well, I'm tired of you, too."

∾

Many good jokes involve W.C. Fields and his supposed love of the bottle. He used to say, "I always keep a bottle of whiskey around the house, just in case I see a snake—which I also keep around the house." Another: "You know I don't particularly like to drink. It's just something to do while getting drunk." And: "I know my capacity for drinking. The problem is I get drunk before I get there."

∾

"Do you know what bosoms and martinis have in common? One's not enough and three are too many." (I tell this joke to make a point on designing golf courses, saying you always have to think of at least two holes and design them in pairs because you have to match up the holes going away from the clubhouse with an equal number coming back.)

～

This burglar breaks into a home. He's shining his flashlight around when it hits upon a Doberman pinscher who's smiling at him with big teeth and eyes gleaming. The burglar thinks to himself, "Oh, my goodness, I've really had it now."

Just about that time, out of the darkness above, he hears a voice that says, "Jesus is watching you." He turns his flashlight in the direction of the voice, and the light hits upon a parrot that says again, "Jesus is watching you." Now the burglar is somewhat relieved and emboldened, so he says to the parrot, "Oh, you dumb bird, is that all you can say?" So the parrot says, "Sic him, Jesus!"

～

Sometimes I use the name of the person who introduced me or enroll the richest person on hand for this joke. Jack says to Jill, "I don't have a big house like Donald Trump, but I do love you and I want to marry you. I don't have a jet airplane and a yacht like Donald Trump, but I do love you and I want to marry you." So Jill says to Jack, "I love you, too, but tell me a little more about Donald Trump."

～

A male chauvinist pig is someone who goes out with a beautiful lady and spends all evening talking about himself, then says, "We've talked enough about me. Now let's talk about what you think about me."

～

Humor can help us all stay young at heart. It's important to add life to your years, not just years to your life. The more we laugh, the more we live, and the more gracefully we grow old. You've probably heard it said that old age is not for sissies. Geriatrics usually enjoy jokes in general, and geriatric jokes in particular. They're able to laugh at themselves which is one of the primary reasons they have become geriatrics.

Like these two 85-year-old ladies in a nursing home...one says to the other, "Don't you think this place is dull? Let's do something to liven it up." The other one says, "Okay, what do you suggest?" The first says, "Why don't we take off our clothes and go streaking?" The other one says, "I agree." So they did. They run by these two 85-year-old men sitting in rocking chairs on the front porch of the nursing home. One guy turns to the other and says, "What was that?" The other replies, "I don't rightly know, but it sure did need ironing."

∾

Or there's one about the 90-year-old man who goes into a house of ill repute in his wheelchair and says to the madam, "Obviously, I'm crippled. I can't see too well. I can't hear too well. I can't smell too good, but I want a woman." She says, "Let's face it, old fellow. You're finished." He says, "I am? How much do I owe you?" Sometimes I think I'm finished too, so I can identify with that old fellow.

∾

You know, the four stages of male senility go like this: "The first stage, you forget names. Second stage, you forget faces. Third stage, you forget to zip up. And the fourth, you forget to zip down."

∾

A parting shot...
There's a well-versed litany about how alcohol affects men in general. The first drink that a man has makes him think, in

his own mind, he's witty and charming. The second, brilliant and articulate. The third, rich and famous. The fourth, tall, dark and handsome, and a good dancer. The fifth, affectionate and irresistible. The sixth, invisible. And the seventh, bullet-proof.

The first time I heard this particular litany, I attempted to validate it that evening. After the party, my wife Nancy asked me, "Robert, has anyone ever told you that you're witty and charming and devastatingly attractive to the ladies?" I said, "No, honey, they haven't." To which she replied, "Then why in the world did you think you were all of those things tonight?"

I sometimes think that God invented golf...and wives...to keep men humble.

NICE & EASY

It's nice to be important, but more important to be nice. It's easy to be nice when life's going good and you're feeling fine. The bigger challenge comes when you're down and out. It takes a bigger, better person to be nice when you're tempted to be just the opposite. Sometimes, I've found that it helps to simply remember and repeat the Golden Rule: "Do unto others as you would have them do unto you." What the Golden Rule doesn't say is also profound. If you follow an approach to life to just be nice, life gives back to you.

6

Just Be Nice

Being nice comes natural when I put my brain in gear before I put my mouth in motion. When I'm guilty of letting my mouth take off before my brain can catch up, it usually spells trouble. Like Benjamin Franklin said, "The heart of a fool is in his mouth, but the mouth of a wise man is in his heart." Remember when you were little, your mother would say, "Now, play nice today and share your milk and cookies with your friends." Maybe it's been awhile, but the advice is still good. It's like the sign behind my desk that reads, "Keep your words nice and sweet, just in case you have to eat them." We've all been there, and unkind words always taste worse than nice ones. I try to say something nice or nothing at all. That's another piece of wisdom our mothers usually tell us, isn't it? Anyone who just thinks in terms of "I, me, and mine" all the time turns inward and becomes like a prune—hard as a rock on the inside and shriveled up on the outside. I don't know about you, but I have enough trouble looking good without being compared to a prune.

Through the years, I've received dozens of letters saying that I have done nice things for other people. They include notes from students who were Dedman scholars to correspondence from total strangers who had heard one of my talks. But I don't have to keep their letters to know that I just enjoy being nice. Sam Walton at Wal-Mart said he'd like to be remembered "as a good friend to most everyone whose life I've touched; as someone who has maybe meant something to them and helped them in some way." Sam was one of my favorite heroes and became a role model to me. I first got to know him several years before I went on the Wal-Mart board of directors and then even better for the six years I served before his death in 1992.

Sam always impressed me. Obviously, he created one of the biggest fortunes in the United States and probably the largest retail empire the world has ever seen. And he did it all by being brilliant, creative, and innovative, but also with a tremendous work ethic and humility that was genuine. He had a real talent for just being a nice, commonsensical, down-to-earth human. He had to be a success with his brains and attitude. Sam also possessed another talent that I thought was sensational. He was always giving someone else the credit. I don't think I was ever around him when he didn't thank somebody else for something they had done, or brag on them for something they had done. Just being around him was a thrill because he was such a humble, talented, and considerate person.

∽

Of course, having friends means being a friend first. One of the real blessings of Nancy and my marriage is the number of thirty-, forty-, and fifty-year friendships we have. Our marriage has been much more enjoyable and enduring and our lives made richer because of these long-time friends. We have several couples with whom we have partied, traveled, and celebrated birthdays and anniversaries together. Some are our tennis and golf buddies like

Jack and Jayne Dale, Ace and Jayne Black, John and Mary Watson, Jim and Lois Williams, Peter and Edith O'Donnell, Bill and Rita Clements, Ed Cox, Bobby Stewart, Gene and Kathy Bishop, Bayard and Corky Friedman, John and Helen McKinley, J.B. and Dottie Fuqua, and many others. We've taken cruises to Alaska and around the British and Greek Isles with the O'Donnells and Clementses. We also have newer friendships we enjoy very much, especially those we met in Horatio Alger. But to mention all their names would take up the rest of the book.

≈

I think the nicest thing anyone ever did for me came by way of a guy named Jim Fenner. We were fraternity brothers in the Tejas Club at The University of Texas at Austin. He loaned me $800 to buy a used car and told me to pay him back if and when I could. I really needed that car to get a job. He did what he did for me, strictly out of friendship. Two years later when I tried to pay him back with 10 percent interest for the whole time, he took the money but not the interest. I've always considered him a genuinely nice person to do something like he did for me.

I believe the world is full of nice people. We don't read about them as much as we should. We don't see or hear about what they do all that often, or often enough, but nice people do exist. I find great comfort in knowing many nice people. Many more, I haven't met, but I do know they exist. Being nice is really a way of life. It's how we touch others in a positive way. Being nice is how you wish everybody else was. It's how you aspire to be, especially when you're not. Being nice just feels good. If it feels bad, it's probably not nice. Always try to avoid giving anyone the justification to say to you, "I thought creatures like you rattled before they struck."

It's so important in life to learn how to diffuse situations, and not get into arguments for the sake of having arguments. There's a quote from the Bible that reads: "A soft answer turneth away wrath. Harsh words stir up anger." We should all remember to disagree without being disagreeable. It's nice to be able to disagree and be nice doing it. There was this reporter interviewing a one-hundred-ten-year-old man, who asked him his secret to such longevity. The old man says, "Well, I've never disagreed with anybody in my entire life." The reporter was obviously caught off-guard, so he says, "Oh, come on now. There has to be more to it than that." And the old man says, "You could be right."

Being nice is more than actions. It's an attitude. Being nice is more than giving material things or earthly resources to this person or that cause. It's the giving of your time...our most cherished possession. Being nice is offering a shoulder to cry on, a heart big enough to share a burden, or two ears willing to listen to someone else's problems while forgetting your own. Dr. Norman Vincent Peale, who co-founded the Horatio Alger Association in 1947 to honor contemporary Americans who have achieved success and excellence in the face of adversity, once said: "Empty pockets never held anyone back. Only empty heads and empty hearts can do that." Some of us have more money than others, but we all have heads...and hearts. Receiving the Horatio Alger Award was a very emotional moment for me because Peale always has been a hero of mine. I am inspired by rags-to-riches stories about people overcoming adversity and equally inspired by the youths who receive scholarships from the association. These kids come from incredibly difficult circumstances to become scholars. I find it very heart-rending, but also emotionally rewarding, to hear their stories.

∾

Being nice also means having a sense of community and respect for the environment. Very early on in the company, we started a program at all of our country clubs that encourages members to buy live trees from us—for less than they could buy cut trees—to use as Christmas trees during the holidays. Then they could plant them in their own yards or return them to us to plant on our properties. In fact, I wish every garden club in America would push this type of program. To me, it's tragic to celebrate the birth of Christ by cutting down millions of trees. In addition, dehydrated cut trees become a fire hazard. Every year, there are more deaths from house fires during Christmas week than any other week of the year. Just think, it takes twenty trees to reoxygenate the carbon dioxide from one car. Life is livable in the cities in direct proportion to the number of trees in them. Wouldn't it be nice if Christmas were celebrated every year by moving millions of evergreens from the rural areas of America to the cities? Surely the Golden Rule includes being nice to nature and ourselves.

∾

Sharp-edged words are only capable of erecting walls between people, but words of encouragement and appreciation have the power to build bridges. As a people, we suffer from a growing shortage of sincere appreciation these days. There are hundreds of critics around, eager with anticipation to tear someone down, but the person who takes the time to commend and encourage is all too rare. This philosophy extends into the business world and continues to be the basis for the operating principles of ClubCorp. It has, in a way, become a primer, something I might label "Private Clubs 101," which has taken shape as a variety of ways to recognize and reward our employee partners.

"The Strawberry Program" was initiated by an employee partner to foster positive attitudes through employee recognition. When a staffer or a club member felt that someone had done a job especially well or performed a noteworthy service, they'd fill out an "Add-a-Berry" card. The berries were then tallied and at a certain level, the employee would get a paid day off. Our two highest awards were the President's Pin and the Chairman's Pin, which included a personal visit to the club by the president or myself to honor the employee. One year, Bob Johnson, then president of CCA and now president of the ClubCorp International Group, went to Houston to present a President's Pin to the locker-room attendant at Kingwood. It was on a Tuesday, and the weather was horrible. Because of the unusual sleet and snow, he didn't expect very many to show up at the presentation. But to his surprise, every member of the club's board of governors braved the terrible weather to recognize and honor that locker-room attendant. He was their guy. That's the kind of thing that has allowed us to retain dedicated and loyal employee partners and to make a club a club.

∾

Another technique that I use and recommend is to distribute "warm fuzzies" at the beginning of each day. When we have 20,000–plus employee partners, there are bound to be quite a few people doing things right. If you'll write them and tell them so, you know it makes them feel good. It makes them feel appreciated, and they realize, "Hey, I'm with a pretty good outfit." The net effect helps build morale, encourages teamwork, and cements their own pride in what they do and where. This practice also serves as a good example of what others need to be doing.

One of the best ways to build people is to recognize and praise what they're doing right. Kenneth Blanchard's book, *One Minute Manager*, says to walk around your office to catch someone doing something right so you can praise him or her. Don't, as some managers do, walk around to see if they can catch someone doing something wrong. I don't send out as many "warm fuzzies" as I should, but when I do, I know the notes are good for the recipients. They put them in their personnel files. They show them to their families and co-workers. And I get a boot out of sending them too. I start my day off right with something good, a living example of a positive outlook with a smile, as opposed to a bunch of problems and nothing but frowns.

It's easy to just react to problems. It's much harder to anticipate problems before they need solutions. One of the biggest problems in business is that, by and large, the only problems that finally get to the top are those that aren't solvable at a lower level. They're the kind of problems that are almost endemic, that you just have to wrestle with for a long time. You're presented with problems that someone else in the organization hasn't yet been able to resolve. That can make it lonely, negative, and frustrating at the top, if that's all you ever look at. It's better if you can budget your own time and find something that's fun to work on. That's why I think that a chief executive officer of any company ought to be primarily a cheerleader. Cheering others on is precisely what the CEO should do, but obviously there's more to it than that. The "cheerleader" must communicate a vision and goals for the company and make sure that people come together to do all of the things necessary to achieve them.

$$\infty$$

Every organization progresses in direct proportion to the degree it builds good people. So we're not only in the club business. We're primarily in the people-building business. I usually conclude my "P-L-A-N" talk, which ends with "being Nice," by quoting two famous philosophers. One is Yogi Berra and the other, Plutarch. Both of their quotes revolve around decision-making. Yogi said, "When you come to a fork in the road, take it." Obviously, what he's saying is when you're faced with a decision to make, make it. Don't waffle. Don't back away from it. If you do, either circumstances or someone else will make the decision for you. If you have a fork in the road and take either one, you have a fifty-fifty chance of being right. If you stand there and do nothing at all, you have a 100 percent chance of being wrong. The longer you stand there, the greater chance you have of getting run over. And no matter how important any decision is, it's usually just the beginning of a series of decisions. The more important a decision is, the more that seems to be the case. You seldom decide right the first time. But as soon as you start down the road of a decision and see that it needs to be changed, the sooner you can do it and, the better off you are. Even taking the wrong road. Because the faster you know you're on the wrong road, the faster you can go back and take the other fork.

The other philosopher that I quote is Plutarch, who said, "Only a fool learns from his mistakes. A wise man learns from the mistakes of others." Then I add, "A brilliant man not only learns from his mistakes and the mistakes of others. He also learns from what he's done right, and perhaps more importantly, from what others have done right." You can learn more from positives than from negatives. You can learn more from something that's been done right than from something that's been done wrong. When you make a mistake, all you know is what didn't work. You still don't know what will work. That's one of the reasons we get educations, to know how to do it right the first time. Emerson said, "Hitch your wagon to a star and you will go very far." That's why everyone should have role models to emulate to know what has already worked.

People who rise to the top are decisive. Even if they're wrong, they don't waffle about decision-making. In my opinion, President Harry Truman was the epitome of decisiveness when he decided to drop the atomic bomb. The buck stopped there, and he knew it. There's another president story about Lyndon Johnson. One day, LBJ reputedly went into a livery stable in his hometown of Johnson City. The blacksmith had placed some horseshoes on the hearth to cool off before he put them on the horse's hoof. LBJ reached over to pick one up and the blacksmith said, "Mr. President, those shoes are still pretty hot. I wouldn't pick them up just yet." Well, LBJ picked one up and dropped it immediately. The blacksmith smiled and said, "See, I told you." LBJ smiled back and said, "No, it just doesn't take me very long to examine a horseshoe."

Even if you're not president, the road to success or failure is a product of the quality of your decisions. That may not sound very profound. But the quality of your decisions can be drastically enhanced by improving the quality of your decision-making technology. If you'll go through a certain litany in making most decisions, you won't make as many mistakes. In a company, when a chairman comes before a board with a problem, he or she should say: "Here's the problem. Here are the salient facts bearing on it. Here are our alternative courses of action. Here is my recommended course of action." If it takes the board more than one-fourth as long to say "yes" as it did for the chairman to go through that litany, then there is a bigger problem than the one you are talking to. A chairman works at least two hundred to two hundred-fifty hours a month with staff support. The board usually meets only two or three hours a quarter so if it has to substitute any part of that litany, the problem's bigger than it seems. You obviously have the wrong chairman or the wrong board or the wrong idea of their proper, relative roles. I constantly tell our executives at ClubCorp that when they're working with a subordinate, force him or her to go through that same litany: Here's the problem. Here are the salient facts bearing on it. Here are the alternative courses. Here is my recommended course of action. Hopefully, all the manager has to say is, "I agree." The more chairmen can manage their companies that way, and just say "I agree," the more they're surrounding themselves with good executives who know how to make decisions. And the better the decisions should be, because they're being made by those closest to the problem.

In any business, there will be times when people disagree over what needs to be done. The important thing to remember in those situations is to be able to disagree without being disagreeable.

∾

Back when I was general counsel for H.L. Hunt in Dallas, I remember being in his office about 7 o'clock one evening after everybody else had gone home. We were talking over some business when Dink Dalton, the head of Placid Oil, called in from Shreveport. Mr. Hunt said, "Dink, how'd it go today?" Dink said, "Not so good, H.L. It's been a pretty bad day. We lost a well. Sadie Zoller put a tool in the hole upside-down and we couldn't fish it out, so I let him go and we're having to drill another offset well." Mr. Hunt said, "Why did you let Sadie go?" Dink explained that he felt like Sadie's mistake was so horrible, the only course of action was to let him go. Well, I remember Mr. Hunt saying, "Dink, hasn't Sadie been a real good hand all through the years?" Dink said, "Yep, he's been one of the best tool-pushers we've ever had." Mr. Hunt thought a minute and then said, "Dink, I think I'd go try to get Sadie back if he'll come back, because he's probably the only man we have in our whole company who won't make that mistake again."

No one is perfect, but everyone possesses some good, even lovable traits. That goodness needs to be recognized and fed as often as possible in all of us. Author Lewis Carroll wrote a fantasy about a lock that keeps running around in distress, crying, "I'm looking for someone to unlock me." This little story may sound strange, but we should try to keep this picture in our minds. Many people need a key to unlock them. They need someone in their lives who will bring out the talents that are locked within them. I was impressed recently when my granddaughter, Christina, showed her tender side. Nancy and I were babysitting and she said to Christina, "You're being so careful helping Jeffrey up the stairs. How come?" Christina replied, "Nanna, Jeffrey's very important to me." We were both impressed with Christina's kindness toward her little brother.

George Eliot, a famous novelist and poet, once said, "I not only want to be loved, I want to be told that I am loved..." The biggest disservice we render to ourselves and to others is when we feel inclined to compliment and encourage someone, but we remain silent. The confidence that someone else has in us just might be the only missing ingredient to encourage us to do what we otherwise might be afraid to try. The gift of encouragement can change a person's life. In 1875, Alexander Graham Bell traveled to Washington, D.C., to arrange for patents. During his trip, he visited Joseph Henry, the director of the Smithsonian Institute, who was very enthusiastic about Bell's theory for telegraphing speech. But in the course of the conversation, Bell admitted he did not have the necessary grasp of electricity to develop the theory. "Well, then," barked Henry. "Get it!" Later, Bell wrote to his parents, "I can never tell you how much those two simple words encouraged me." Those two words changed his life.

When it comes to offering your encouragement, never hesitate. Even Mother Goose knew the importance of being nice. She said, "Good, better, best; never rest till 'good' be 'better' and 'better' best." Being nice. Encouraging others. Doing either is the best way to be the best. In my book, it's the only way.

A Club Is...

I guess this would be a good time for true confessions. We once had an obnoxious and foul-mouthed member at Brookhaven who was always griping about something. I decided we were either going to cure him or get rid of him. Others were insisting that we do something. So I wrote this poem called "A Club," framed several copies of it and had them placed in two or

---

three conspicuous places around the clubhouse. It goes like this:

A Club

A club is a haven of refuge and accord in a world torn by strife and discord.

A club is a place where kindred spirits gather to have fun and make friends.

A club is a place of courtesy, good breeding, and good manners.

A club is a place expressly for camaraderie, merriment, good will, and good cheer. It humbles the mighty, draws out the timid, and casts out the sorehead.

And a club is one of the noblest inventions of mankind.

The poem was signed "St. Andrews, Scotland," to give it a sense of historical importance. The impact wouldn't have been quite the same had I signed my name to it. After all, St. Andrews, the first golf club in the world, was founded in the 1600s in Scotland. My plan worked. The poem's "reason for being" was in the catch phrase—*cast out the sorehead*—and it helped everywhere. The poem was so club-like that it seemed to bring people together. We even had a competitor put it on the front of his club's menus!

In a high school picture from 1944, I'm wearing my Outstanding Speaker in the Nation pin (and my "elephant ears"). *Photo courtesy of North Dallas High School Viking Yearbook*

BOB DEDMAN
Birthplace: Rison, Arkansas
Viking Editor; **Compass** Proof Editor;
"Senior Pub" Feature Editor; Four-
Year Linz Pin; Everts' Award; Linz
Bible Awards; First Place Texas
Latin Tournament; National Foresnic
League Degree of Distinction; City
Debate Representative; Second Place
Debate Tournaments; First Place
North Dallas Extemporaneous Tourn-
ament; Debate Letter; Original Ora-
tory; First Place City, District, Divi-
sion, Third State in American Legion
Oratorical Contests; Kiwanis Radio
Play Contest; First Place Essay Con-
tests; Presidencies: Latin Club, De-
bate Club, Homeroom, National For-
ensic League, Junior Classical
League; National Honor Society;
Civic Federation Representative;
Perigon Club Secretary; Baseball
Team; Tennis Team; Literary Letter
Sweater; National Student Congress
Senator.

My senior year accolades in the North Dallas High School Viking yearbook.
Photo courtesy of North Dallas High School Viking Yearbook

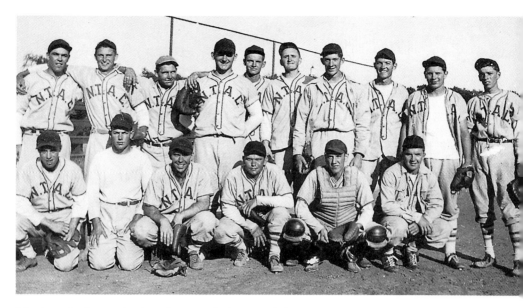

That's me in the catcher's uniform with the rest of the Naval Air Corps baseball team at The University of Texas at Arlington, Texas (then it was called North Texas Agricultural College), in 1944. *Dedman Photo Collection*

Notice my biceps and shoulders in this one! I'm the first one on the left on the bottom row with my baseball teammates in the Naval Officer Corps at The University of Texas in Austin, 1946. *Dedman Photo Collection*

What a difference 40 years makes! After Brookhaven opened in 1958, all of our employee partners gathered on the grounds for this photo. Today, we would need a much bigger field to accommodate all 20,000-plus ClubCorp employee partners worldwide. Photo by William Langley

Talk about the middle of nowhere! Here's an aerial view of Brookhaven, ClubCorp's flagship club, under development in 1957. Notice the lack of homes around the club. That's all changed now. *Photo by William Langley*

That's me at the top of the photo presiding over a pow-wow of top ClubCorp executives in 1965. *Dedman Photo Collection*

Jackie Gleason had us all in stitches at our Inverrary Country Club during the Inverrary Classic in 1976. Gerald Ford, my wife, Nancy, and I enjoyed the laughs. *Dedman Photo Collection*

Entrance to Robert H. Dedman Memorial Hospital in 1981.
Photo courtesy of Dedman Medical Center

Son Bob, Nancy, daughter Patty, and I were all smiles at the dedication of the
Dedman Medical Center in Dallas on August 18, 1981. *Dedman Photo Collection*

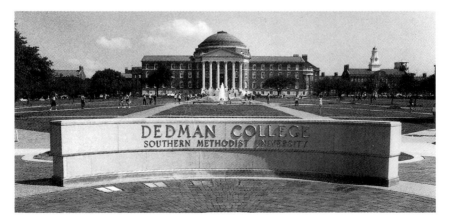

The day that SMU named the College of Humanities and Sciences after our family
in 1981 was one of my proudest. *Photo courtesy of Southern Methodist University*

Blessings in my life have been many, like my grandchildren. We now have three. My first, Jonathan, came with me to the company picnic in 1984. *Photo by Charles Thatcher*

I don't really know if I was helping or hurting in this tug-of-war at the ClubCorp picnic in 1984. It could have been both. *Photo by Charles Thatcher*

I was flying high when this 1982 article was written about my first stint as chairman of the State Highway and Public Transportation Commission for Texas. *Cover photo courtesy of* Texas Business *magazine*

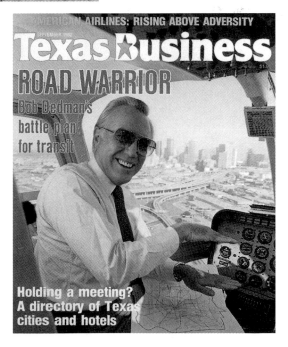

AMERICAN AIRLINES: RISING ABOVE ADVERSITY

Texas ★usiness

ROAD WARRIOR
Bob Dedman's battle plan for transit

**Holding a meeting?
A directory of Texas
cities and hotels**

When a group of ClubCorp
executives in Dallas gave me a
rose for every year for my 60th
birthday, I stopped celebrating
birthdays. That was 1986.
Dedman Photo Collection

My emotions ran high when I accepted
the Horatio Alger Award in 1989.
Dedman Photo Collection.

I was honored to be in such company at the Horatio Alger Awards ceremony in
1989. Included among the recipients and their presenters is J. B. Fuqua (back row,
second from left), who introduced me. I am on the first row, second from left.
Dedman Photo Collection

Together, Nancy and I have made our house a home. Here, we are sitting in front of the big window in our living room in the summer of 1990. *Dedman Photo Collection*

As chair of the board at Southern Methodist University, I was sure proud of the new SMU president Gerald Turner, who made his first commencement address there in 1995. *Photo by Hillsman Jackson*

In the presence of three great guys—Ernie Dunlevie, the tournament chairman, Bob Hope (with wife Dolores), and Arnold Palmer—I felt humble as the host at a reception on January 16, 1996, honoring the comedian's induction into the Indian Wells Classic Hall of Fame. *Dedman Photo Collection*

ClubCorp CEO and president—and, more importantly, my son—Bob and me in my living room in 1996. *Photo by Neil Whitlock*

What a legend! Following his retirement as head coach of the Dallas Cowboys, Tom Landry and I shared a few strokes in the Tom Landry Golf Tournament at one of our clubs, Stonebriar Country Club, in 1995. Proceeds went to the Fellowship of Christian Athletes. *Dedman Photo Collection.*

The year my wife, Nancy, and I gave our $30-million gift to SMU was the same year ClubCorp turned forty years old. I'm wearing a special pin to commemorate that in 1997. *Photo by Hillsman Jackson*

Nancy and I sported flashy gold sashes on the night the Dallas Historical Society gave us the top Philanthropy Award in 1997. We're the handsome couple on the left. *Photo courtesy of the Dallas Historical Society*

Dottie Pepper, the *real* golfer in the middle, played with four amateur partners in the Pro Am of the J.C. Penney LPGA Skins Game at Stonebriar in 1997. I stood next to her, hoping some of her talent would rub off on me. *Dedman Photo Collection*

Looking good in my gold tassel, I gave the commencement address to graduates at Methodist College in Fayetteville, North Carolina, on May 10, 1998. That same day, the college honored me with a Doctor of Humanities degree. *Dedman Photo Collection*

WIN-WIN

I think one of ClubCorp's secrets to success is the careful selection of the deals we go into and the people we do them with. It takes two things to make a good deal—the deal and the people who come with it. I'd probably trade with the Devil himself if he had something I wanted and we both could come to an arm's length agreement relative to it. But part of that deal would have to be not continuing to do business together. Here's why: With a bad partner, surprises are always for the worst. With a good partner, surprises are nearly always for the better. You can make a bad deal into a good deal if you have a good partner. If you have a bad partner, even a good deal can turn sour. At ClubCorp, we do deals with honorable people who will live up to their end of the agreement. Things always work if you do deals with the right people. They never work if you do deals with the wrong people.

7

The Only Good Deal Is a Win-Win Deal

The phrase "win-win" and I go way back. We share about forty years of history. I know I've been saying it, selling it, and living it for a very long time. "Win-win" always works. At ClubCorp, our record of repeat business is living proof. We've done five deals with Exxon in Houston, Texas—the first of which was Kingwood on the north side of town. We have four golf courses there now and the club's been a tremendous success since the early 1970s. The fact that we've done four more deals with them since then—Deerwood Golf Club, Greenspoint Club, Bay Oaks Country Club, and Clear Lake Golf Club—is the best testimony that our partnership has been win-win for both of us. Exxon has a reputation for being one of the best partners in the world, and deservedly so. They became a huge company by being the best partner. Exxon begins talking about a joint venture with one main objective: "We want to be a good partner." And guess what happens? People practically beat down their door to partner up with them. They enter into every agreement with fair and honorable intentions, and always display the highest degree of integrity that anyone could wish for in a partner. Their approach is setting up a deal where both can win because when they do, both win big. That's been the case with all five of our deals with Exxon. They've been a super partner all the way.

More specific details about two of those deals better illustrate our win-win philosophy. In September 1972, we agreed to develop and operate Kingwood Country Club, a golf course and country club in conjunction with surrounding land developed by Friendswood Development Company (a division of Exxon). Twenty years later, Kingwood is used as a benchmark for successful country club/residential development. With a total membership of more than 3,000, Kingwood now boasts four eighteen-hole golf courses—paid for from the club's cash flow. In December 1990, Bay Oaks Country Club in Clear Lake had a negative cash flow of about $1.4 million. One year after assuming management duties there, we brought the negative cash flow down to less than $400,000 by controlling operations systems and financial management, improving the club's food and beverage usage, and raising the overall quality of services. Within a year, the club had added thirty new members. We then negotiated a purchase agreement with Exxon's subsidiary in December 1991. A year later, the club had added sixty-eight new members with a positive cash flow and has improved every year since.

Deals with other business partners also have been win-win experiences. We've made six or seven deals with Equitable Life in city clubs and athletic clubs through the years. We've had four deals with Ken Schnitzer (chairman of Century Development Corp.) in Houston, seven deals with Gerald Hines of Houston, and three with developer Trammell Crow in Dallas. One with Crow involved a deal over in Hong Kong, twenty-five to thirty-five years ago now. Trammell Crow's partner, Ewell Pope, and I traveled to Hong Kong to look at a deal on Lantau Island, which is now a major development. I'd taken only a small travel bag with me because I thought we'd take a quick tour and return to the States the next day. But it started to rain and didn't stop for two or three days. One of those days, I finally suggested that we go ahead and look at the land despite the rain. Ewell Pope said something to me I've never forgotten: "Robert, you never show land in the rain. Nothing looks worse in the rain than land, women, and chickens."

∞

The club business is no different from any other industry. Clubs have to have everything a successful sales organization does—a good product, skilled management, dependability, reliability, and excellent follow-through—so they can get repeat sales and referral sales. It's a shame that there are some hucksters who think it's easier to steal pennies than make honest dollars. Why go for pennies? It will not lead to repeat business. The fact that we do repeat deals with the same people is the best evidence that past deals have been win-win for both sets of partners.

We're in the repeat-business business. The club members we have, we want to keep, and mainly through them, get others. The members we have are our best source for getting new ones. We have to look after the members we have, and the new ones we get, well enough so they'll want to help us get more members to join the club. We have to do repeat business with our members using their clubs and retaining their memberships. In the deal-making business, we're also in the repeat business. We want to do repeat business with the same people because if we can't, it's going to be hard to do business with others. If you deliberately, or inadvertently, out-trade or oversell people, they'll never do another deal with you—or refer you to someone else. We make every effort to be a partner of choice.

Even when a club is in trouble and it's ClubCorp to the rescue, everybody still wins. The previous owner gets out of a losing situation. Our company grows in size and stature. The members enjoy a better-run, more successful club, and the entire community is enhanced when the golf courses are beautified and maintained to the industry's best standards. And the assurance that the courses will endure dramatically increases the value and marketability of the surrounding homes. Often, this process doesn't take much time. We can quickly turn a losing situation into a winner with our immense purchasing power to buy items like restaurant supplies, golf carts, course equipment, carpets, and irrigation systems—many times for as much as 40 percent less than an individual club standing alone is having to pay for those same items. That's how to run a better club for our members and thereby increase the gross income and decrease the expenses relative to it.

When ClubCorp bought its first resort in 1984, Pinehurst Hotel and Country Club was losing $1 million a year. We upgraded the operations and the marketing of the resort and within a year, went from losing $1 million to making $4.5 million. Within four years after its purchase, Pinehurst was generating an operating profit of $10 million, and we've been re-investing nearly all its profits to further improve it. This is obviously "win-win" for everyone involved—the members, homeowners, employees, area merchants, and the community. It is the site of the next U.S. Open Championship. At ClubCorp, we love the challenge of taking something that's broken and fixing it. Solving problems gives us a rush of sorts. While other people might like to spend their time fretting and lamenting over what they're going to do, we're saying, "Boy, this is fun. Let's figure out a way to fix this and make some money so we can plow it back into the property to make more money for everybody's benefit." We'd like to think we're pretty good at problem-solving. Don't misunderstand, though. We can't possibly make everybody happy all the time, but we sure try. Nor have I ever

The Four P's

ClubCorp's success is based on four factors: People, planning, purchasing power, and programs. We know what the score is, and we know what's possible. When we're buying for 200-plus properties, we have volume purchasing and get a better price on everything we buy: china, glassware, liquor and wine, furniture, carpet, tables, chairs, golf carts, mowing equipment, everything. We know what we ought to pay. We know what quality is and we ought to get a super price. Many times, all it takes to get a 40-percent discount is to say, "What's your trade price?" Most people make more of their money by their good purchasing practices than they do by how much they gross. They are very careful in the spending of the money they earn, and they learn how to get wholesale prices. We're somewhat like the "Wal-Mart" of the club business. We buy better and pass on that greater value to our club members. And everybody wins.

wanted to be a Rhett Butler—you know, somebody who has a propensity for getting involved in losing causes—where deal-making is concerned. Fighting losing causes is not a healthy pursuit in my book. We've made some bad deals along the way, but we sure didn't think that they were going to be bad when we made them. The few bad deals have been the results of misreading the market or the quality and character of the people involved in the deal.

ॐ

People like to do business with us for a lot of reasons. One is our success in the types of ventures they want to do. They like to identify with somebody who's already successfully done what they need done. That's the secret of all successful executive search firms. It's a simple principle—hire somebody who already has successfully done what the client needs. That's one of the reasons why people do business with us, because we've done what they need done—not just once, but many times and with a level of success that's hard to match.

And they like the way we think. They are familiar with our track record of success. They appreciate how we've transformed the club business from "nobody's business" to "our business." With more than forty-one years under our belt, they know we have gotten operations down to a fine—and very profitable—science. They also acknowledge our broad base of members from across the country that can make their club or their deal more successful than it would otherwise be. If we do our job, they'll want to be in our development when they move to another city. They'll want to belong to another one of our clubs and pay fees for that privilege. They'll want to buy more homes around our developments. That's on the club side. On the resort side, if we do our job, they'll keep coming back because they know we'll make them feel like kings and queens. They already know that our standards are set high to exceed their expectations, not just meet them. If this sounds like a sales pitch, it is. We have a lot of edges that separate us from our competitors. It's nice to have competitors because our success, in a way, has helped create them. But people who want to do business with us already know what our strengths are. And we do everything possible to go beyond telling them what they are. We show them.

Sometimes I don't think we're as transaction-oriented as others wish we were. What we do is more like a courtship. We get to know each other. We look each other over, much like a man and woman do when they first meet. We say, "Wow, you're good-looking. I'm good-looking. How much do we have in common? Do you think we could become friends? Now that we're friends, do you want to get married? Maybe it's time to negotiate that prenuptial agreement." If someone wants to build a golf course or sell a golf course or anything else for that matter, we establish a relationship with that person—first. During our courtship, that person starts thinking, "There isn't anybody that I'd rather sell my golf course to." They have almost made up their minds to sell it to us before we ever start talking marriage. For some people, this courtship period can be a little frustrating. They'd rather just ask, "What's your deal?" Or say, "Here's what we want." We respond better to a slower pace. We like to ask, "Why are you selling? What are you trying to accomplish?" Our executives suspect this feeling that goes beyond the sale is one of our biggest success secrets. People don't feel like they're doing a deal with a big company. They are dealing with me or my son or any other of our top-level people. And they see our accessibility in action. They know if they ever need to, they can pick up the phone to call any one of us and say, "Hey, I've got a problem." We'll always do our best to help.

ॐ

The biggest (and best) win-win relationship in my life is my wife Nancy and our forty-five year union. I've always heard behind every successful man is a woman who either inspired him to success, drove him to success, or spent him into success. You'd better believe it! I recently asked a friend and former bachelor, "How's married life?" He said, "Great, now that we've learned how to fight." I think that's a very good observation. It's okay to bite and scratch and carry on with your significant other, but not drawing blood is an important part of getting along together for an enduring marriage. Animals learn how to fight and not hurt each other. People who stay married learn how to do the same thing.

I once heard a toast at a reception for a couple of newlyweds that went like this: "May your marriage always be filled with sunshine and sprinkled with just enough rain to help you grow." Being a good partner is as important to being a good father and grandfather as white space is to words. To really partner up with your loved ones, you have to listen loud. If you're doing something that makes them happy, keep doing it. If you're doing something that hurts or offends them, then try and correct it. To be a loving partner means that your love is abundantly apparent to those around you. That love can take the form of many things. Giving them what they want (within reason, of course). Spending time with them and enjoying them. Playing with them. Showing them that it's fun to be around them by spending even more time with them. Supporting them. Gently coaching and praising when appropriate. Forgiving them. Being there when they need you. All of these traits add up to being a good partner.

❧

Even with such win-win philosophies, there's no doubt about it, starting ClubCorp and developing Brookhaven Country Club were gambles. I had a lot of business savvy, but no prior country club experience. But I recognized a "10" when I saw it. There was a tremendous potential market for members. I had a vision to capture that market and recruited the talented people as partners to help me do what needed to be done. If properly served, I was convinced this was a market that would prosper. After all, people join private clubs because they want to feel special and privileged.

Our members became our partners in lots of unique ways. When Brookhaven was built, the golf course was full of rocks. We really didn't have the money to pay somebody to pick up all the rocks, so the members organized a rock-picking party. We had golf carts going up and down the course completely full of rocks. How's that for proof that they felt like we were all in this thing together? We really did call everybody partners…and still do. Our employees are partners. Our members are partners. Our financial backers and lending institutions are partners. Our homeowners are partners. Developers of the land around our clubs are partners. And even more important, we meant it when we called them our partners. They became our best source of new members. They knew as we grew, they could have a better club.

∾

To succeed, you must give value. Brookhaven was promoted and sold on value. The value in a club (or whatever else we build or buy) is still the most important commodity we have to sell. The need to deliver the finest value for every initiation fee dollar, every membership dollar, every athletic dollar, and every food and beverage dollar was recognized early on. The reason's so obvious to us. With members, everything is possible. Without them, nothing is possible.

We started from the beginning with a concept of giving value in facilities, services, flowers, programming, and self-images. We have always based our "reason for being" on giving value—real value, not the false values of keeping out certain people that other clubs have been based upon. Race, gender, or religion didn't make any difference to us. We based our membership on diversity and personal achievement, and the value both have to offer. I'd like to think we were more in keeping with a modern outlook in America than what the other clubs were doing at the time. This philosophy of giving value enabled us to get a bigger, more diverse membership base, which in turn added more value for our members and employee partners.

We achieved this to such a point that when Israel celebrated its 40th anniversary of becoming a state, one of our members came to my office. Robert Strauss had a prominent reputation as a lawyer, Democrat, and diplomat. He was chairman of the Democratic Party when Jimmy Carter was president and his special ambassador to the Middle East. Interestingly enough, when President George Bush needed to appoint a new ambassador to Russia, he called on Bob Strauss. He's had an important role in Washington, D.C., and national and international politics on both sides of the aisle. Anyway, he came to see me one day and said Israel wanted to honor me with its 40th anniversary Freedom Medal. They would raise funds around honoring me and use those funds to plant trees in Israel. He said they wanted to honor me for two reasons. One was for making a lot of money in the right way, and being smart enough to not only know how to make it but give it away, too. Secondly, we had always taken in members in our clubs based on personal worth rather than false values. Then he turned on his irresistible charm. He said, "Because of your open-member philosophy, you have a lot of Jewish members in your clubs. And because you have so many Jewish members, you can't afford to turn us down." I thought that was a mighty persuasive argument on his part—and excellent use of very few words (for which Strauss is famous).

ClubCorp has always been a family affair. When Bob was about five years old, we were driving out to Brookhaven on this two-lane, country road called Valley View Lane. Barely a stop sign and no stoplights in sight. Brookhaven was finished and going strong. We got all excited because we could see some more homes being built off of Forest Lane in the distance, a mile south of Valley View. Our son said, "Look, Dad. See those homes? That means more members for Brookhaven." I smiled because I was thinking exactly the same thing. Today, he's president and chief executive officer of ClubCorp International, and chairman of the board of ClubCorp of America. He was elected to that position in January 1989. A practicing psychologist, our daughter, Patty, bolstered our Human Resources department in the beginning, still helps out with quality control and currently serves on our board of directors. After her first child was born, she devoted herself more to mothering—she now has three children—and her own counseling business. I asked her once, "Why do you want to have so many children?" She asked me, "Why do you want to have so many properties?"

My wife Nancy, who also serves on the board, did a lot of consulting work for ClubCorp, especially in its infancy and toddler stages. She helped the designers find furniture, art, antiques, china, silver, and other things like that. She has always had very good taste and is extremely knowledgeable about what I call "couth." In fact, she has always been affectionately referred to as our vice president of, and secret weapon in, couth. She played a part in the design standards and quality criteria for many of our clubs. She knows food and beverage extremely well. Having studied with great chefs around the world, she'd actually proofread our menus in both English and French. She had a good manner about her of keeping everybody on their toes in a nice way. And her talents represented quite a savings to us while ClubCorp grew in sheer numbers and types of clubs.

∾

Win-win relationships remind me of the Biblical verse, "The only thing we ever really have is what we give away." For me, win-win has become more addictive than all the vices of life. It's something to be shared. Once I felt it, I never wanted to lose the magic. It's something to be cherished. Making sure everybody wins is an experience that's worth repeating. It's a lot more rewarding than being a loser. Born losers are those who win at the expense of others. Winning is just something they think they know how to do, but those of us who enjoy creating win-win relationships know the real truth. Nobody cares what you know until they know you care.

THE GIFT OF GIVING

In today's world, we are forced to dwell on too many negative thoughts and moral decay, all of which points to our country as having seen better days. Every day, more than two thousand teen-agers drop out of school. Three million children are abused every year. Four out of ten children live in single-parent households. Although we do have our share of problems, there is still much good in this great country and a tremendous showing of people who want to make it better for others. The heartland of America is not in one geographical location, but in every one of our fifty states. Some say, give until it hurts. I say, give until it feels good. And whatever you give comes back to you many times over.

8

They Don't Put Luggage Racks on Hearses

I don't know if I originated the phrase, "They don't put luggage racks on hearses," but I first uttered those words on April 2, 1981, in explaining our $25-million gift to Southern Methodist University in Dallas. Nancy and I were at a gathering to celebrate being part of the largest single gift ever made to SMU, and as such, we became distinguished as the givers of one of the largest personal gifts in the history of American higher education. Former SMU President L. Donald Shields made the announcement of our gift and Edwin L. Cox, chairman of the SMU board of trustees, called the occasion "one of the greatest days in the history of the university." I am proud to have played such a positive role in SMU's history. I felt even more honored when the board recognized us by changing the name of The College of Humanities and Sciences to the Dedman College of Liberal Arts on May 8, 1981.

Both of those days were emotional for the entire Dedman family. To this day, I remain grateful for the university's honoring us in such a significant manner, and even more important, I was thankful to be alive to enjoy the moment. There's no doubt—

having a college named after us in our lifetime is an emotion-packed experience. And although others occasionally have accused me of being an overly-emotional guy, I prefer to consider myself as "sincerely sensitive." I willingly acknowledge my high appreciation for nice things and goodness, such as love, affection, and super-achievers. I believe in and enjoy everything that's good and don't apologize for either. The long-legged, beautiful dancer Juliet Prowse played tennis at our house one Sunday afternoon and said she would never want to go out with a man who didn't cry. I can see why.

In my opinion, if you can't show your emotions, you turn inward—and become what I call "kinda crusted" on the outside. You really cannot relate to others too well. I'm thankful that it's easy for me to get emotional, especially when I read a meaningful poem or tell a good story or joke. And when I see a collection of ClubCorp executives who are good-looking, talented, and extremely bright, my eyes swell up with tears. My voice has a way of cracking—and they're onto me right away, sometimes teasingly, but they know I'm real and my emotions are genuine.

When the folks at SMU asked me to put some of the feelings behind our gift into words, it was a tough assignment. I was laboring under several handicaps—emotion being only one. The fact is, I'm much better at money-making than I am at speech-making. Not to mention the humbleness I felt speaking to that group on that day. The biggest challenge was that it was like preaching to the choir. Everyone assembled that day believed very deeply about SMU and was assiduously working in its best interest. Obviously, Nancy and I love SMU or we wouldn't have done what we did.

I just prayed for the right words to express some of the reasons that led us to make the commitment we had made. It was my sincere hope that our thinking might help these dedicated educators to clarify their own thoughts, and possibly give them some ammunition to use in encouraging others to do as much or more than we did (or certainly the maximum, according to each individual's ability). I must admit, however, that I was intrigued by the number of people who commented more on the motives behind the gift rather than the amount of the gift itself. So I talked about the "why's" on that day and SMU later polished my thoughts into a pamphlet entitled simply, *Why?*

∾

The first "why" naturally is: "Why philanthropy?" Or, "Why give to charity?" I've come to love answering this question. To do so, I rely on the biblical injunction, "To those to whom much is given, from them much is expected." The late John F. Kennedy had his own version: "For those who much is given, much is required." It is easy to become imbued with the main thought behind both statements. But there are a few factual considerations for practical people to keep in mind when discussing philanthropy. Fact one: The older you get, the more you realize that you can't take it with you. I humorously tell people I have tried to figure out a way to do just that, but have not come up with any solutions. They really don't put luggage racks on hearses. Another fact: When you die in this country, the estate taxes are horrendous—more than 55 percent, to be exact—if you have much money left in your name or much of an estate and don't give it away. It doesn't take a rocket scientist to know that an estate can disappear by a tax as high as 55 percent. I first learned this lesson during all those years as a young tax lawyer in estate planning.

That brings up the next question: "Why give it away while you are alive?" Well, there are several reasons. The easiest answer for me comes from the enjoyment, the literal thrill of giving while living. Most of us have worked for a lifetime, so it's downright fun to see some of the fruits of the orchards we have worked in while we are still alive to enjoy them. I know I enjoyed the experience of the SMU gift much more than I will my own funeral.

The more practical reason to "give while you live" is to encourage others and to help them decide it's the right and responsible action. In addition, you have the opportunity to monitor your gift and see what is being done with it, if you give away a significant portion of your estate while you're still alive. If you wait until you are dead to be a benefactor, you don't get another turn at bat. There is no way for you to rectify any mistakes with the balance of your estate.

The most difficult question to be resolved involves the selection of a particular charity. Well, what could be better than education? Someone once told me, if you invest in a crop like corn or cotton, you invest for a year. When you invest in oil or cattle or timber, you invest for several years. When you invest in education, you invest in forever. In my case, I'm greatly indebted to education. My roots, as I have related, were humble, giving me first-hand knowledge that a good education is the best tool to help someone lift himself or herself to a new level of life. I am a product of our educational system, so I happen to think it is a good one. I went to college four degrees' worth. That fact speaks more eloquently than any words I could craft on paper as to the high priority education has in my book. Education not only helped me to succeed, but instilled in me a sense of values to know that money is more valuable if you do something with it. I enjoy being able to put something back into the system that contributed to my success. That fulfillment is what prompts me to give. Being able to give away $25 million made me more ecstatic than the people at SMU were to receive it.

∾

Our first gift went to private education, which leads to the next logical "Why?" Nancy and I believe strongly in the need for both tax-supported institutions and private institutions. Public education and private education counterbalance each other. However, the survival of private education is much in doubt. At the end of World War II, the number of students in higher education was equal in both private and public institutions. That ratio has now dropped to fewer than one-fifth of the students in higher education being enrolled in private institutions like SMU. The very survival of private education is threatened, in my judgment. Society would incur a terrible injustice if we did not have a viable and, quite frankly, growing private sector in higher education. If higher education were solely under the auspices of politicians and bureaucrats, the basic freedoms we hold dear could be in jeopardy.

Another concern of mine revolves around the synergistic, symbiotic relationship between private and public education. The only seeming rationale for students' paying more money to go to a school like SMU rather than to a tax-supported, and considerably less-costly school, is that a private education is perceived as better. Thus, private institutions must deliver an education of sufficient high quality that justifies the costs. If we citizens want an alternative to the tax-supported schools, we must commit to the continuing goal to help the private institutions be better. Ultimately, we achieve a double-barreled effect: By swinging a leverage to uplift private education and raise its quality, we also help improve the quality of public education.

I first focused on SMU because every member of our family believes it is the finest asset of Dallas. It's one of the principal reasons that Dallas is such a superb city in which to live and work. SMU also is our whole family's alma mater (our foster mother). We all graduated from there. So it just made sense to give to our alma mater, if we're going to push education. Nancy and I selected the College because we feel the humanities and sciences serve as the heart of SMU. We believe in a balanced education. A university is a college that is surrounded by individual schools, not just a college or professional school standing alone. I've said this many times before: The more we can offer a balanced education, where students can better understand literature, history, psychology, anthropology, theology, and the mental discipline that comes from the mathematical sciences and foreign languages, the better they will be in their chosen fields. It doesn't matter if that profession is law, business, engineering, theology, teaching, or any of the other individual disciplines. A balanced educational foundation enables students not only to do better in their vocations, but also to live life more fully and to learn to better appreciate all that the universe has to offer. That appreciation is the most important impact that any university can have on its students.

So on that April day in 1981, I said that I was somewhat reminded of the Sermon on the Mount. When Christ came down from that sermon, he picked twelve apostles from approximately five hundred disciples. I noted the distinction that "disciple" comes from the Latin word *disciplina*, a follower or discipline; whereas the word "apostle" comes from the Greek word *apostos*, which means a man with a message, one that will go forth and spread the gospel. I knew everyone gathered that day already was a disciple. In my happiest dream, I told them, I wanted us all to become apostles, to go out and tell the university's story, and to deliver SMU's campaign goal over the hump by the end of that year. I said I hoped our gift was not an ending, but a beginning, and that our gift would serve as a pump primer to tantalize many others to accomplish what we could collectively as apostles.

❧

When people ask me how I'd like to be remembered, I usually say, "As a giver and not a taker." The complete answer, however, is more complicated. Saying "a giver, not a taker," is just a good starting point. Givers are people who make the world go 'round better in every way. As a rule, they surround themselves with other givers, and collectively they make things happen for the good of many. They build institutions. They help businesses or industries to prosper and grow. They volunteer their time for the benefit of others. Givers are usually attracted to and surround themselves with other givers. Together, their good deeds multiply exponentially.

Takers, as a rule, have a difficult time attracting anyone other than fellow takers. They become surrounded by a bunch of takers with their hands out. They don't maintain lasting relationships because they tend to take advantage of their partners or associates. The losing party, of course, terminates the relationship, whether it's boy-girl, man-wife, employer-employee, doctor-patient. The actual relationship really doesn't matter. When either partner takes advantage of the other, the relationship isn't going to continue. The end is inevitable. The only question is when. That's why I believe so strongly in the win-win approach to any partnership.

One of my favorite observations is that givers just look better. Really. Just take a look. They usually have smiles on their faces, their lips turn up, and they're a delight to be around. Takers frown a lot, their lips turn down, and they're a big "pain," if you know what I mean. That age-old expression, "You reap what you sow," may be worn, but it's true. Indeed, the concept itself is ageless.

∾

Some around Dallas may have noticed that I've also tapped medicine as another primary beneficiary of our giving. Dedman Medical Center and RHD Hospital in Dallas also bear our family name. Since I've related my viewpoint on private education, perhaps I should explain my interest in medicine and public education. Medicine is a worthy charitable cause because it helps heal

> ## Strikin' It Rich
>
> I'm fond of the supposedly true tale about a West Texas oilman. He was covered with oil from a gusher that had just hit. Reporters were crowding around him, asking what he was going to do with all of his new-found money. He said, "I'm going to divide it into three equal piles. I'm going to spend one-third of it on women, another third on booze, and just waste the other third." I won't fault him—it was his money. I just know what works for me and heartily suggest it might equally work for you. Being a giver, I have found, is infinitely more rewarding than being a taker.

the sick, and after all, good health is one of life's biggest blessings. Medicine is the primary resource available when we need to restore our health. Such pursuits as exercise, moderation, a well-balanced diet, and cutting back or eliminating sugar, tobacco, alcohol, fats, and salts help maintain good health. So does preventive medicine. The healthier we are and the longer we stay that way, the better we all do. But when you get sick, you have to rely on medicine to get well.

Nancy and I are also underwriting eight hundred Dedman Merit Scholars at The University of Texas in Austin. They are the top 1 percent of the students in the University. They are like assistant professors in the classrooms and in campus life. As better students, they help attract better professors and other better students. This is the age of knowledge, or, as I like to call, "the age of brains." No company, no community, no state, no nation is going to do better than the "smarts" of its people. The University of Texas at Austin is the best public university in Texas. I have three degrees from there and Bob and Patty have one each.

I believe the same line of thinking holds true for our more recent philanthropic efforts involving public education. The healthier and the smarter individuals are, the better off all of society will be. Those who work the hardest and learn the most are going to do the best. That's the reasoning behind the establishment of our scholarship fund at North Dallas High School. The scholarships will send four students annually to SMU tuition-free. Not many of the students knew my name or recognized my face when I visited my alma mater to announce the gift. After they heard the words "free," "college education" and "SMU," however, they understood the opportunity and were asking for scholarship applications before I ever left the building.

As a member of the North Dallas Class of 1944, I took great pleasure in returning to the school. Walking its halls, I found myself reminiscing about debate tournaments, baseball games, and four years of grueling Latin classes. I noticed that the minority ratios had shifted over the years, where the current student body is about 80 percent Hispanic and about 12 percent African American. Many of its students come from poor families whose parents didn't attend college, so they don't have a clear concept of what college is. They haven't been told that they can go to college and still work…like I did.

Scholarship recipients are chosen by North Dallas and SMU officials. They must be in the top 10 percent of their class with an "A" average to be considered as a Dedman Scholar. They also must have taken at least two advanced placement courses and be actively involved in school and community activities. Each scholarship represents about $17,600 per student per year. The first recipients enrolled at SMU in the fall of 1998. As a privately-funded effort, this program is a good way for SMU to recruit top minority students. It is my sincere wish that similar programs will spread to other schools in the Dallas area and throughout Texas. The seeds have been planted. Let's see if they grow.

∾

I don't really know if I like being tagged as the "richest guy in golf." I guess it makes for good headlines, but I now prefer to concentrate more on what I can do with money rather than its accumulation. A farm joke from Arkansas contends that manure is quite useful when you spread it around. If you just pile it up, though, it smells horrible. My advice to any up-and-comer in business is to be as intelligent in giving money away as you have been in making it. I've already given away millions, and hopefully have much more giving to do while I'm still on this Earth. It seems like the more I give away, the more I have left.

The American Benefactor magazine listed Nancy and me among the one hundred most generous Americans in its Fall 1997 edition. Also in 1997, we were recognized as the top philanthropists in Texas by *Texas Monthly* magazine for giving away $33 million (in major gifts) in 1997. The magazine classified major gifts as more than $1 million and included the donor's name and the amount given. Some of those gifts went to support programs, scholarships, or building funds at the University of North Texas in Denton, Texas; The University of Texas at Austin, Florida State University in Tallahassee; and Southern Methodist University. The gifts are consistent with our interests, such as the endowment of a chair in club management at the University of North Texas. The Florida gift, too, will focus on the hospitality industry by helping to construct a new building for the College of Business' Department of Hospitality Administration. At SMU, a challenge grant will help build the Dedman Life Sciences Building, which will house SMU's biological sciences department, state-of-the-art research facilities, and classrooms for the natural sciences.

Everyone must come to their own terms with the prospect of giving back to society. Some people follow a philosophy in life to "live fast, die young, and leave a good-looking corpse." It seems like, the more we give, the more we have left. Life really does give back. I'm living proof that givers can thrive on relationships in which everybody wins. The ability to have long-term relationships, to attract repeat business, or to re-invent favorable experiences comes with being a giver. Sure, takers sometimes win, but it's usually just one time and then it's over. They create their own hell. In contrast, givers create their own heaven on earth. All you really take with you when you leave this Earth are the fond remembrances in the hearts of others of the things you gave away while living, including love, friendship, kindness, understanding, forgiveness, and, obviously, material things, too. When you're a giver, your life is rich—full of laughter, enjoyment, and generosity. These rewards come from having givers around you that keep you smiling and having a good time throughout the day. What else can I say about takers? Well, I've heard that Hell is exceptionally hot.

IT'S SPELLED I-N-T-E-G-R-I-T-Y

I heard an insightful story told by a young fellow who got hooked on playing "Monopoly" with his grandmother. She was normally a sweet, kind woman, but every time the playing board came out of the box, his granny took on an uncanny ruthlessness. She grabbed all the property she could. She monopolized the railroads and utilities, and became every player's worst landlord nightmare. She always won. As the fellow grew up, he played better, and, on this particular day, was about to beat his grandmother at her own game. He had become what he had admired in her all those years. In fact, his was sure victory when something else happened. It came time to put the game back in the box.

When I heard that story, I thought, "That's a very important lesson in life. When it's all said and done, everything goes back in the box." Unless…you realize that you are unique. All of us are unique, but many die copies. You must have the tenacity to make a difference in other people's lives. What you accomplish in that process gets too big to fit back in the box. The only things you can really take with you are the fond remembrances of others for what you have done or given away while alive. The lasting impressions you've made don't die with you. What you've meant to others will never go back in the box.

9

What Money Can't Buy

I thought about starting this chapter by listing what money can buy, but there are too many "trappings" you can enjoy in this lifetime. All it takes to acquire them is the ability to pay the purchase price. In other words, money—sometimes, lots of it. As someone who can afford almost anything, I must offer this word of caution about possessions. You don't own possessions. They own you. Given the extent of what is available today, I prefer to concentrate on what money can't buy. Let's start with integrity, honesty, courage, patience, perseverance, self-confidence, love, loyalty, friendship, and humility. In an era where the motives of people with position and purse strings are subject to intense suspicion and constant public scrutiny, some view me as an enigma. I've been a salesman, chief executive, lawyer, father, grandfather, philosopher, humanitarian, company founder, literary scholar, philanthropist, and even served two challenging stints as a Texas Highway Commissioner. I'm supposed to be a walking hundred-dollar bill. Instead, I'm a bold contradiction to the "J.R. Ewing's" of the world. I didn't arrive where I am by destroying someone else. I traveled through life by trying to be a good, decent person.

I don't flaunt what I have done or even brag about what I intend to do. People who are puzzled by "Robert Dedman" don't know me. That's why so much of what I do causes them to shake their heads and wonder, "What's in it for him?"

The first time I read *Hamlet* and memorized Polonius' advice to his son Laertes, I found the answer to that question:

> And these few precepts in thy memory keep. Those friends thou hast, and their adoption tried, grapple them to thy soul with hoops of steel; But do not dull thy palm with entertainment of each new hatch'd, unfledged comrade. Beware....Neither a borrower nor a lender be; for loan oft loses both itself and friend.

To achieve these things is balance at its best. Then Polonius speaks to his son about integrity:

> See thou character. Give thy thoughts no tongue, nor any unproportioned thought his act. Be thou familiar but by no means vulgar. Give every man thy ear, but few thy voice. Take every man's censure, but reserve thy judgment. This above all: To thine own self be true, and it must follow, as the night the day, thou canst not then be false to any man.

Or to paraphrase the 18th-century Scottish poet Robert Burns: "Oh, *wad some power the good Lord give us, to see ourselves as others see us.*" In other words, look into a clear mirror every day and see who you are. Don't delude yourself. Integrity comes from a Latin word meaning wholeness. Integrity means being a whole person and being honest in everything you do, including assessing yourself, good and bad. Always choose the hard right over an easy wrong.

Early in the years of developing ClubCorp, I had the chance to make a deal with the Teamsters on a venture in Las Vegas—with one little catch. All I had to do was pledge Brookhaven, our first and flagship country club, to guarantee the deal. No matter how attractive that deal might have seemed at the time, I wasn't going to take that gamble. I could have legally done it, but, in my own mind, I could not morally do it. I firmly believed I had a moral obligation to protect investments made by the members of Brookhaven in their homes and their memberships beyond their abilities to protect themselves. Being a good steward was more important than making a dollar. ClubCorp probably would have grown faster had I been willing to borrow money on the clubs we already had in order to finance new ones. But it would not have been good stewardship.

∽

To me, being honest starts with self-assessment, in order to see yourself as others see you. For if your mirror isn't clear and you can't see yourself, how can you possibly see others for what they really are? In discussing concepts of value, I can attest there's nothing in the world worth more than good health, family, and friends. I debated about how much detail to go into about my health. Suffice to say, "Stay healthy." I have been incredibly healthy most of my life or I wouldn't have been able to put in the eighty-hour weeks, play as much golf and tennis, or pursue the many other activities I have. I seldom get colds, flu, or such common ailments. I have had some experience with disease but I believe you can overcome most afflictions if you keep healthy and maintain your stamina. If I hadn't been healthy, two or three of my bouts with disease might have killed me. The important thing is that I didn't bring ailments on myself because I was unfit. I don't want to belabor any bad breaks I may have had or play myself up as being a martyr or as immortal. I was fortunate enough and healthy enough to somehow overcome health challenges and, in the process, substantiated my belief that most illnesses are self-induced.

Much of the poor health that plagues society today begins with what we do or don't put into our mouths. Too much sugar. Too much tobacco. Too much alcohol. Too much cholesterol or fats. Too many calories. Statistics show that 80 percent of all illness is caused by one of these offenders. Exercise is especially important in maintaining good health. At ClubCorp, we set up "SLASH STAFS," a diet and exercise plan designed to motivate its participants to stay healthy. We encourage our employee and member partners to ask themselves, "Can I cut out or reduce Sugar, Tobacco, Alcohol, Fats, and Salts?" In other words, how can they "SLASH STAFS?" The program also helps them evaluate their progress. For $50, they receive a physical examination, including blood tests that measure cholesterol and triglyceride levels. This information is recorded and maintained on a small card with columns for their weight, blood pressure, and other blood indicators, followed by spaces for personal goals and quarterly updates. The regimen also requires at least thirty minutes of vigorous exercise every other day. Participants are monitored weekly. Some of the clubs have discontinued or modified the program.

∼

Most ClubCorp club dining facilities also offer "Heart Healthy Cuisine," a menu low in sugar, salt, cholesterol, and other contributors to heart disease. The program is a good step, but self-discipline is the key. If people refrained from smoking, drinking, and unhealthy eating, the gains in productivity throughout society would be impressive. Heart disease research, for example, shows that many people already have their hearts 20 percent occluded at age twenty, 30 percent occluded at age thirty, 40 percent occluded at age 40, and so on. Clubs are in a position to encourage and help people stop that progression. Maybe the answer is preventive medical care. Perhaps the fastest approach to good health—and the most realistic—is moderation. To have a high energy level, you have to do several things. You have to get 56 hours of rest each week and eat properly. In my opinion, you can't drink too much, you shouldn't smoke at all, and above all, you must exercise regularly.

Of course, after such lofty advice, I must plead guilty. I don't exercise as much as I should, and sometimes I probably drink too much. My father did, too. Although I lived with my aunt for about two years when I entered North Dallas High School, my folks later moved to Dallas and I lived with them on Travis Street before I graduated. At times, my dad and I would argue about his drinking. My mother had started drinking when I was still living at home in Rison. I believe the drinking reflected my parents' frustration with the fact that their "ship had never come in."

As time passes, however, my reminiscences of the harshness of those days have softened. Despite my parents' shortcomings, they were people of high integrity. My father was a reasonably good-looking man and what I'd call "a real straight guy." He was always the gentleman, opening doors for the ladies, and never cursing or telling dirty jokes in front of them—even when he had had too much to drink. He served his country in World War I and told stories of being gassed. After the war, he lived with his family in Brownwood and went to Brown Junior College. In his late twenties, he went to Arkansas to try to put an oil drilling deal together. That's when he met my mother. She was probably seventeen when they were married. I was born in 1926 by the time she was eighteen. Mother was born in Rison, too. As a child, I was unaware of my mother's physical beauty—I just loved her—but I recall that my friends would say to me with clear admiration, "Your mother is so pretty."

My dad drifted from job to job as he sought his elusive fortune, and, as I have related, we moved frequently. We stayed in Rison until I was about two-and-a-half years old, then moved around in Texas to Dallas, then Grand Saline, then Tyler, then Lindale, back to Tyler, back to Dallas, then to Rison, Arkansas, and back to Dallas. In our first move to Dallas, we lived in a boarding house that was run by my dad's stepmother. His real mother had died and his father had remarried. I had diphtheria while there. When I was three, we moved to Grand Saline. It was also a year of frequent tornadoes. With each threat, Mother would herd us into a storm cellar filled with canned fruit and vegetables—and long-legged spiders and possibly snakes—to wait out the storm. As kids, we didn't know whether to be more afraid of the tornadoes or those spiders or snakes.

I also saw "Dub," one of the young boys who worked with my dad at a car dealership, perish in an airplane crash there. Dub owned a small airplane and loved to fly. On Sunday afternoons when the weather was good, people from the community would gather at this small landing strip and watch Dub fly. One particular Sunday in April, his plane started to rock out of control, then went into a spin and crashed into the ground. Watching all that as it happened was pretty traumatic for everyone, but especially the little kids. I was only three when I saw "Dub" die and learned a poignant lesson in mortality and not taking unnecessary risks before I could even count to ten.

ॐ

My childhood took place in a different sort of environment from the one in which most people live now. Nowadays, people have bathtubs, hot and cold running water, and indoor johns that flush whether they live in the city or the country. Almost all the cooking in those days was done on a wood stove and one of my jobs was to get the kindling and firewood to help make the fires. Most of the fires were for cooking or warmth, but I remember a woman who lived across the street from us in Lindale, Texas, who would make soap in one of those big black metal pots with the wood around the outside and all sorts of pig lard and lye boiling and bubbling inside. Yes, things were quite a bit more primitive in those days!

Even taking a bath once a week was a chore. I think families with more affluence had No. 3 washtubs, while the poor people like us had No. 2 tin washtubs. You could get your legs into a No. 3 tub, because its larger size was more accommodating to limbs. No. 2 tubs, however, were only 22 inches in diameter, so your legs, as you grew up, would hang over the side. I know the actual size because my assistant has a No. 2 tub that she uses as a firewood bin in her garage and she measured it for me. In those days, we just tried to take a bath as fast as we could. If we happened to live where there was a faucet, we'd fill a bucket with regular tap water first. If not, we had to draw water from the well. Then we'd heat water on a wood stove or a gas stove until it began to boil. We'd then pour it into the tub together with a second bucket of cold water. We'd usually bathe in the kitchen because the floor was either bare or covered with linoleum. That way, the water that sloshed out of the tub didn't matter much. Most people would take baths on Saturday night, so they'd be clean to go out that night or to go to church on Sundays.

∾

Yes, my folks were good people, who had integrity, but they were frustrated. Mom's frustration probably came from my father's drinking and just wanting more for herself and her children. At the time, I was sometimes judgmental and bitter about it. I'm not anymore. When Dad died, I talked to his preacher about borrowing a line from a Browning poem called "Andrea del Sarto": *"A man's reach should exceed his grasp or what's a heaven for."* He thought that was a brilliant idea because that one line described my father well. He was going to Heaven, all right, and his reach had always exceeded his grasp. Perhaps his ship never came in, but his goals were always high. He was constantly putting together the next drilling deal—the one that was going to hit. I understand that now. And I understand the importance of integrity.

Because I wanted to put Arkansas far behind me, I didn't see my family there, including my younger brother and sister, from the time I graduated and went into the Navy until after I was married and had two children—the time from when I was eighteen to almost age thirty. It didn't even occur to me to invite them to our wedding. I regret to say that it was almost as if they didn't exist, like there was some kind of Freudian block in my mind. After Nancy and I had children, we would take them to visit their cousins in Oklahoma. As they became older, they started asking, "What about your parents? What about our other grandparents?" So I called my parents and Nancy and I took the kids to see them. We started a dialogue, saw them several times, and reached what I'd call "good accommodations" before my success came when I was thirty-one or thirty-two. Then I helped them and bought them a house. Eventually, I became close with my family, unusual perhaps, considering the distance between us at one time. The reunion was ironic in ways. Dad had quit drinking because he wasn't in good health. He died shortly after we celebrated my parents' 50th wedding anniversary. Mom joined him about a year later.

∾

One of our biggest rewards as parents is seeing our children grow up and try to be as good—or even better—parents. Today, Patty and Bob are both serious about being married and part of a family. We're reaping those rewards now because they love to spend time with us, and we love to spend time with them. We have a ton of photographs showing us doing everything in the world together—hiking, biking, fishing, golfing, you name it. Patty frequently takes her kids on trips with us because she remembers what she and Bob got out of our travels. We go to The Homestead and Pinehurst once or twice a year, to Aspen in the summertime and to Barton Creek in Austin for long weekends, just to be together and spend time with her kids.

Our children have helped us to be good grandparents. They're facilitators, if you will. They realize the importance of our spending time together and encourage us—and their children—to make it happen. Loving, caring, having fun with your children will ultimately help them want to be with you and share their children with you. When it all works out that way, you just can't beat it.

Money can't buy a great relationship with your grandkids. They renew our hope, recapture our youth, and help restore our faith in the whole system. Seeing a child conceived by our children lets us witness the whole scheme of life at a time in life when we have time to enjoy them. We can play such an important role in their lives. It's a role that should be taken seriously, because we have so much that we can give. With babies and toddlers, we can be an additional source of love and care. For school-age children, we can teach family values and history. We can inspire older children and adolescents to want to grow up and be just like us if we perceive ourselves as good role models. But to do that, we have to be a constant and consistent presence in their lives. Grandparents and grandchildren already share a natural affinity because they have a common enemy—the parents who are between what they want to do and what they can do. Both grandparents and grandchildren often perceive the parents as being the biggest part of the problem. What most young

parents really need from their own parents is sympathetic support, not advice and criticism. One of the hardest jobs for a
parent—and a grandparent—is making a child realize that "no"
is a complete sentence. While it's sometimes painful to watch
your children go through the trial-and-error of parenthood, it's
part of their learning curve. It's best to let them know that we're
there for them if they need us. We're eager and willing to listen.
We're glad to offer the wisdom of our own experiences if and
when they want it. And we'll babysit every chance we get!

I'd love to be able to give my grandchildren what my parents
and poetry gave me. One of the great things about parents is that
they help you to distinguish between what really matters and
what doesn't matter in life. My parents tried to teach me that,
and poetry picked up where they left off. For me to have the
chance to give that knowledge to the children of our children, is
almost better than anything else I could possibly accomplish.

But I've already told you more than you want to read about
being a grandparent and spending time with my grandkids.
Nancy's mother told me one time that she saw an old friend in
Phoenix and she asked her, "Did I ever tell you about my grandchildren?" The woman replied, "No, and I appreciate it."

∾

When it comes to what money can buy, I must admit to one
weakness. Historically, my biggest extravagance has been shoes. I
didn't have real shoes for most of my childhood. Instead, I often
wore pasteboard shoes that would crater almost instantly. I'd glue
rubber soles on them, but they'd never stay glued on and they'd
go flap, flap, flap when I walked. Eventually, I'd just go barefoot,
and that embarrassed me. Today, I have a number of alligator
shoes, ostrich boots, and other fancy shoes—numbers, in fact,
beyond what makes economic sense. Maybe I thought if I ever

made enough money to afford really good shoes, then I was going to have them. And, of course, alligator shoes can be resoled, and they don't go flap, flap, flap when I walk. They always look shiny and new, they last for years and they look so good for so long. Maybe that's why I have so many shoes—they never wear out anymore. Another possession that conjures up memories was my Navy officer's overcoat that I kept for many years. It was so heavy, I never wore it. That old thing probably weighed at least 50 pounds, but I wouldn't let go of it, just in case hard times came back. Believe it or not, my biggest fear for years was being poor again.

I'm Honored . . .

Abraham Lincoln said, "*Honor is more important than honors.*" I have had the distinct pleasure in my lifetime to know many great men and women, and what's more important, the honor to call them my friends. At the same time, they've bestowed numerous honors on me, as friends tend to do. I received the Entrepreneur of the Year Award for Texas in 1976. I was named Dallas Humanitarian of the Year in 1980 and admitted into the Texas Business Hall of Fame in 1987.

In addition, the Northwood Institute in Michigan once named me as Outstanding Business Leader in the Nation. My education friends closer to home also have been good to me. I've received the Distinguished Alumni Award at The University of Texas at Austin and the Distinguished Alumni Award at Southern Methodist University. The 69th Legislature of the State of Texas passed a resolution in my honor on May 24, 1985, to commend my "exemplary record of public service to my state."

I am truly grateful for every plaque, every statue, and every

---

kind word ever spoken about me. And you can take that to the bank.

I joined a host of other fine people as a recipient of the Horatio Alger Association Award in 1989. Some of their stories are extraordinary and I wanted to share them with you.

∾

Tom Harken, self-made millionaire and founder of Tom Harken & Associates. Harken has given hundreds of speeches on battling illiteracy in America. His inspiring story began with a childhood marred by a serious bout with polio. He remembers getting sick to his stomach one night in his iron lung, but he laid there in his own sickness and cried all night...until a doctor came to help, cleaned him up, and then hugged him. He's said that he will never forget the comforting smell of that doctor's starched white coat.

Tuberculosis was Tom's next childhood challenge. He was quarantined in his room for almost another year. His mother would leave food by his door, and his father wrote "I love you" in the snow outside his bedroom window. Illness had kept Tom from attending much school, so when his classmates constantly teased him about his illiteracy, he quit. He dropped out of school in the seventh grade and went to work for his father. And Tom was a hard worker. He sold shoes part-time, then vacuum cleaners, but he had to memorize the necessary details and relate them later to his wife, "Miss Melba," who filled in the blanks on his sales forms.

In the 1960s, he started selling recreational vehicles and soon became the nation's top independent RV broker. He then purchased one Mexican food franchise and soon grew into Casa Ole's largest franchisee. In 1992, he was awarded the Horatio Alger Award, an honor that he labeled "the Oscar, the Emmy, and the Tony of real life." Only ten out of hundreds nominated each year receive the award. Tom was overwhelmed to be next to other 1992 winners like Supreme Court Justice Clarence Thomas and Henry Kissinger. That night, the audience stared at Tom in shock as he told his secret, the same one harbored by millions of

Americans. Until recently, he'd been illiterate, he told the crowd. Miss Melba knew. So did a finite few others, but not many people. Even his two sons didn't know. When they'd climb into his lap and beg him to read to them, it was all he could do to keep the tears from flowing. Miss Melba always came to his rescue, though, saying, "Daddy's tired; let me read to you." The whole audience gave Tom a standing ovation for his unbelievable story and uncommon courage.

The next year at the 1993 Horatio Alger Awards ceremony, Henry Kissinger told him that he only remembered five speeches in all his years of political life. Tom's was one of them. Since that night in 1992, Tom has given hundreds of speeches on battling illiteracy in America. His main message is, "All you have to do is ask, 'Will you help me?'"

One more comment about my friend Tom…he received his high school diploma thirty-seven years late as part of the Class of 1992 at his alma mater in Lakeview, Michigan. He'll give you a big smile today when he talks about his personal library because he can read anything his grandchildren ask him to read.

∾

J. B. Fuqua, who created one of the greatest fortunes in Georgia with Fuqua Industries. The Fuqua School of Business at Duke University is named after him. He's another Horatio Alger Award honoree who knows the meaning of win-win. ClubCorp bought Inverrary Country Club—the longtime Florida home of golf's Jackie Gleason Classic—from him in 1975. It was losing a lot of money when we acquired it but almost immediately the property started making good money. J.B. was so impressed with what we accomplished at Inverrary that he invited me to serve on his Fuqua Industries board of directors.

I asked him to talk to our executives at one of our retreats, and his was one of the best speeches I've ever heard. He is a genius at analyzing deals and making them work. I served on the Fuqua Industries Board of Directors for several years, and saw the evidences of his entrepreneurial spirit first-hand. It's very appropriate, I think, that he gave enough money to Duke

University to have The Fuqua School of Business named after him. I know he goes back there and gives an occasional lecture. I'm sure the students learn a tremendous amount from him. He has a component at the school that is actually helping a lot of Russians learn how to do business better and restore their country's economy. That just sounds like something J.B. would do.

∾

Sam Walton, the late Wal-Mart founder. Sam created probably the largest retail empire the world has ever seen and served as one of my all-time heroes for many reasons. He was a genius at purchasing, expense control, and loss control that enabled Wal-Mart to be the lowest-cost provider in the retail industry, and by virtue of being the lowest-cost provider, the company also became the largest organization in sales that the retail industry has ever known.

It was so interesting in board meetings to hear Wal-Mart executives explain how they had been able to cut the cost of sales for any number of reasons, such as loss control, expense control, or mass purchasing. They seemed thrilled to add: We can now reduce our prices some more. Of course, that meant they would get a bigger market share and make even more money. They literally did perceive themselves as purchasing agents for their customers, which I felt was a very wholesome outlook. If you can deliver the best buy to the customer, you'll do the best. Which is the essence of America and the essence of why Wal-Mart has been so phenomenally successful.

∾

Dr. Robert Schuller, Crystal Cathedral Ministries founder. Robert is the best minister I've ever known and another person I admire very much. He's a super preacher and gives his congregation the best example of a self-help attitude by saying, "If it's going to be, it's up to me." He is also a master at encouraging people to set goals by repeatedly preaching, "If you can dream it, you can do it." He has millions of people in his audience every Sunday, which speaks for itself. Not only that, he keeps the audience interested and he keeps it growing. He preaches a delightful gospel, about a bigger God than many denominationalists want to acknowledge.

∾

Dr. Norman Vincent Peale, the author of *The Power of Positive Thinking*, had one of the largest media ministries of all times and co-founded the Horatio Alger Association with educator Kenneth Beebe in 1947. They had hopes of recognizing and honoring contemporary Americans who have achieved success and excellence in the face of adversity. I was inducted into this prestigious collection of courageous men and women in 1989. It was truly one of the greatest honors of my lifetime.

Each year, the Horatio Alger Association hosts career, public service, and community service seminars, as well as sponsors free-enterprise conferences, conducts internship programs, and awards almost $1 million in college scholarships annually. These scholarships are given to high school seniors who have already faced adversity in their short lives, yet have risen above it and achieved excellence. Horatio Alger Youth Seminars reach almost 100,000 students across America, allowing them to meet previous award winners face-to-face and talk to them one-on-one. Young people realize that the American Dream is available to anyone who's willing to make the journey.

∾

Ralph Waldo Emerson once wrote, "*Hitch your wagon to a star and you'll go very far.*" A whole galaxy of "stars" in my life have engendered my personal admiration and respect. Some of them are famous. Some aren't, but they all shine brightly on my horizon. I only wish I could have mentioned them all here.

SELLING FUN

There are all types of fun, and a thousand and one different ways to have it. Playing any sport. Going to the movies. Taking your kids to the zoo. Riding horses on the beach. Kissing your sweetie in the moonlight. Well, you get the idea. I have tons of fun playing golf and tennis. Lamar Hunt used to tell me, "You have more sayings than anybody I've ever met," then added insult to injury by saying, "You're the only person who, while playing tennis, will get your mouth tired before your legs."

10

Are We Having Fun Yet?

At ClubCorp, we're in the business of selling fun. When we formulated the twenty "Basics" on how to run our clubs and passed them out to our employee partners in the field, they came back and said we had forgotten to include the most important one: Having fun. The more fun we have, the more money we make. The more money we make, the more fun we have. I'm probably the luckiest man alive because my work is literally my playground. So often in life, what people do for a living is a chore. They have very little fun in earning their keep.

Now that I'm seventy-two, I still usually work more than forty hours a week. In all honesty, though, it's hard for me to call it work because I enjoy what I do so much. For that matter, that's been true for my entire life. I've always had a ball, like that bricklayer who was building a cathedral, not just making $14 an hour. Having fun is my final "Rule of Order" but the real challenge is striving to live up to all ten. I feel that I have, because these rules represent the "how's" and "why's" of my moderate degree of success in life. There's no limit on what you can achieve or how much money you can make, if you follow them in business, too.

∾

The question about which came first—the chicken or the egg—
is a little like people asking me which came first—golf or
ClubCorp. I played golf before I created this business of golf and
long before I was tagged "the richest guy in golf" by *Golf Digest* in
1996. I was about a five handicap before I started ClubCorp, so I
obviously played a great deal of golf before I went into the business of selling fun. After golf became both my vocation and avocation, I made it a point to do a little work on Saturday mornings
and then play golf Saturday afternoons. I'd do something similar
on Sunday: Go to church, work awhile, and then play golf.
There's a saying in the golf industry that anyone who shoots
more than 100 hasn't any business on the course. He should be
taking some lessons so he will enjoy the game more. But anyone
who shoots under 80 has no business. People in-between are
looking after their business and their golf game in the right proportion.

Along the way, I would manage to play several sets of tennis a
week. Now, I often substitute tennis for weekend work. My "business" golf sometimes gives way to time on the links with Nancy
and my grandson Jonathan on Sunday afternoons. And it's still
impossible for me to pick the sport I like best.

One of the beautiful things about tennis to me is the total
involvement that comes from the movement, the physical
activity in hitting the serve, the running to the net—all the
moving around. Players sustain a vigorous pace almost all the
time. It's an aerobic pursuit, as well as a game. It's also psychological. Hitting the tennis ball itself is a good way to get rid of hostilities or frustrations. It's definitely better for someone to be
hitting a tennis ball than taking out frustrations on their loved
ones. Or yelling at their executives. Or forgetting to be a friend.
Or sucking on a bottle of vodka. Or popping a bunch of pills.

There is another addictive advantage to tennis: Your opponent. In golf, you're really not playing an opponent. You're playing the golf course and matching scores with someone else also playing the course, which are totally different pursuits. Tennis, however, is about the joy of contest, evoked by every game and aroused by every stroke. I love the game and its surroundings, and their effect on my mind and emotions. Golf is a game of space; the tennis court is a cage by comparison. In tennis, you play people. In golf, you play the course.

The beauties of golf, of course, are in the eye of the beholder and being outdoors with others for a long period of time. Golf provides a collage of images: hills, valleys, a gleaming lake in the distance, birds and other animals, hospitable clubhouses with verandahs and armchairs, shower-baths, tea and toast, whiskey and soda, companionship. The delights of the game also include the great breeze that greets you on the hill, the whiffs of air that come from green things growing, the wet smell of fallen leaves in autumn, the hot smell of pines at noon, the sense of freedom on a great expanse of green hues, the flowering trees and plants, the exhilaration, the vastness, the exaltation. You see nature at its best in the birds, squirrels, rabbits, and deer as you breathe deeply and take in the sun.

❧

There are other comparisons and incongruities in the games of golf and tennis, which lead to deeper discussions and add to the fun. In his book, *Confessions of a Hooker*, Bob Hope wrote: "I get upset over a bad shot just like anyone else. But it's silly to let the game get to you. When I miss a shot, I just think what a beautiful day it is. And what pure fresh air I'm breathing. Then I take a deep breath. I have to do that. That's what gives me the strength to break the club." Golf is a very demanding game in itself. You always think you're going to whip it, but you never do. Golf is a little more frustrating than tennis. You can relieve hostilities and frustration by hitting a tennis ball and sweating and all. Golf will build up frustrations because you never play as good as you think you should, if you take it too seriously. In fact, part of its intrigue is you cannot understand why golf is such an addiction. The challenge of golf is one reason people—old and young alike—keep coming back for more. Every course and every hole of every course are new mountains to climb. It's an incredible game, and so is tennis.

In golf, the mental exercise usually outpaces the physical achievement. The allure is unceasing; the fascination, endless. You always can imagine a longer drive, a more accurate approach, a more certain putt; never, or rarely ever, do you effect all three on many holes of a round. But all golfers live in hopes of accomplishing that elusive confluence.

I like everything about golf. I like the courses, the green grass, trees, flowers, lakes, squirrels, birds, just being outdoors. I think that we have a subconscious feeling in ourselves that we want to get out and play like kids in wide open spaces, which you don't get to do much at my age. Golf is one of the few ways to do that. I like the challenge of golf because it's you and the course. I like the discipline of golf. I noticed that the majority of the pros at the U.S. Senior Open at Pinehurst in 1994 checked their grip. After playing as long as they have—all of them more than thirty years and most of them more than forty years—they're still checking their grip, one of the basics of the golf set-up.

∽

I go on about golf because the game truly is a metaphor for life. You don't have to be a golfer (although it helps) to understand that the game involves keeping score, hoping to win, and learning to lose. In any given round, you get some good shots and some bad ones. You learn balance from the exaltation of good shots and the dejection of bad shots, and learn to accept both with the equanimity I extol in *Keeping Your Balance*. I like the concentration that golf requires because it diverts your mind from problems. I like the fun of being with various partners. Men and women. Children and grandchildren. It's just plain, healthy fun to be outside, competing and enjoying each other. And thanks to the handicapping system in golf and the different tees, you can make it an equal game with golfers of varying skill levels. Everyone can play his or her game and have a good time.

Many times these days, I'll play golf with my grandson Jonathan. It'll be just the two of us playing between groups of foursomes. Instead of just waiting intermittently to hit a shot (because twosomes are going to be faster than foursomes), I'll play two balls and play the best ball. Or we'll play a "scramble" where I'll hit two balls and he'll hit two balls and we'll play the best ball of the four. That encourages him to become a better golfer. Playing scrambles is a growing trend in golf and I believe one of the reasons for the game's rise in popularity. A scramble is where everyone hits a tee ball and then all play the best ball of all the shots. Beginners can hit from the forward tees, so partners often will play their tee balls. Then they'll have a chance to hit to the green on the third shot because their partner's ball is likely to go farther than theirs. This way, they'll learn to chip, pitch, and putt. They feel like they are really playing golf instead of being out in the woods looking for their balls. Sometimes, when Jonathan and I are playing a scramble and I've hit an unusually good shot—one I couldn't possibly beat with a second shot— he'll say, "Granddaddy, don't hit a second shot and risk the chance of proving the first shot was an accident." How'd he get to be so smart?

ॐ

Part of the fun of golf that we try to instill at our clubs involves the game's rich history—although not all of its traditions. Golf, after all, is a game with a shady past and its actual birth is shrouded in mystery. Golf cannot point to a legal father, such as baseball in the case of Abner Doubleday or basketball in the case of Dr. James A. Naismith. There's a question whether golf was ever born at all or if it just evolved from the game that was played on the moors of Scotland in the fifteenth century. I heard once that golf came from signs posted, saying "Gentlemen only, ladies forbidden," but I've never been able to validate that statement. We certainly practice just the opposite at ClubCorp. We've been trying to get women, juniors, seniors, and beginners into golf, and initiated such efforts from the very founding of the company.

∾

I've been lucky enough to have played golf with some of the best and most fascinating people in the world. Pro-golf legend Byron Nelson is one of my all-time favorite partners. He was the first director of golf for us at our first club, Brookhaven. Not to mention he was an incredible golfer, teacher, and human being. Aside from being a super guy, he has set records in golf that many believe will never be approached, let alone equaled or surpassed. In 1945, for example, he played in thirty tournaments and won an incredible 60 percent. And of the eighteen tournaments he won that year, eleven came in a fantastic streak, from March 8 through August 5 with a scoring average through all eleven tournaments of 67.31. That's incredible, considering the balls, equipment, and course conditions in 1945.

I also played quite often with Ben Hogan, who some say was the greatest pro golfer who ever lived. That was in the early days of ClubCorp when we did some consulting for two years for

Shady Oaks, Hogan's home course in Fort Worth. He also was a good teacher and a fun person to be around.

Another fellow with whom I played frequently was Ralph Guldahl, our golf pro in Los Angeles when we started Braemar Country Club in 1959. He had won consecutive U.S. Open Championships in 1937 and 1938 and then held the scoring record at the Masters for many, many years. He could play tremendous golf. A financing agreement in conjunction with Braemar required that I spend three days a month in California, so I usually had the pleasure of playing with him a couple of those days each trip. Ralph probably taught me more about scoring than anyone. One time, legendary golfer Sam Snead and Ralph were playing what's called a Scotch foursome, which means they were hitting alternate shots. Sam always outdrove Ralph about thirty or forty yards, so he said to Ralph, when he was having to hit one of Ralph's shorter drives, "Ralph, how do you short-hitters ever win a golf tournament?"

I'm sure I'm not the only one, but I could talk forever about Sam Snead. He's a fun guy. His favorite course, I think, is the Upper Cascades course at The Homestead where he grew up playing. He lives in Hot Springs, Virginia, now and, although he's in his eighties, he shoots even par on the Cascades course. The last time we played, we played from the white tees, but Sam can still hit the ball. I played with him one time in Florida when he was seventy-six. He said, "Bob, I'll give you twelve shots and play you a $20 nassau from the back tees." "Okay," I answered. I had a 79 for a net 67, and he shot 66. He had a hole in one and a couple of eagles that day, and beat me by one stroke and won $40. He was six strokes under par for the day and beat his age by ten shots. He's an incredible athlete.

The last time we played, I asked Sam, "If you only had one bit of advice to give a golfer, what would it be?" I thought the message would be something about the turn or swing because he's

> ### Just for Fun
>
> I've always had a "both-and," as opposed to an "either-or," attitude toward life...and in business. Since I play a lot of golf and tennis, people ask me which one I like best. I really never say because I like both of them equally. They both have different qualities. It'd be like asking you which one of your children you like best. You like them all for different reasons. People wonder which business I like best: city clubs or country clubs or athletic clubs or resort clubs. I like them all. I don't perceive that they exist at the expense of each other. I think you should develop every line of your business just like every child you have—to his or her maximum individual potential, and not at the expense of the other deals or the other children.

always had such a big turn and a long, fluid swing. And that's why people called him Slammin' Sammy Snead. His reply was about the grip. "People ought to make sure that the V's on both hands touch all the way to the thumbnail on both hands, and both of these V's point to the right shoulder," Sam said. It was amazing to hear a guy who has won more than eighty tournaments, talking about the importance of the grip so eloquently. It's the grip that I use, by the way.

॰

Just in case you're wondering, I played tennis and golf with several presidents of the United States. And, yes, I had fun—and gained much fodder for my storytelling. I played tennis with George Bush, although I don't remember playing golf with him. I did play golf with Gerald Ford, who used to play at the Inverrary Classic. We played there in the Pro-Am and on Pinehurst No. 8 when we opened the course in 1995. Then, in 1996, three presidents played at our Indian Wells Country Club in Palm Springs.

Ford and Bush and Bill Clinton teamed for that round. I didn't get to play with them, but I visited with them in the locker room afterward. I think among them, they bagged three spectators in the first round of the Bob Hope Chrysler Classic. Bush had the lowest score, but the most hits. He first hit Norma Earley on the nose, causing a cut that needed ten stitches. He apologized; she did, too. "I'm sorry I got in the way of your shot," she offered. Bush later hit John C. Rynd in the leg and Ford hit Geraldine Grommesh's finger. Neither was badly hurt. The male spectator that Bush hit later said Ford would make a great baseball player, commenting, "He uses all of the ballpark." Bush and Ford scored 92 and 100, respectively. President Clinton was reportedly disappointed in his score of 93, calling it his worst round in years.

∾

Fun is what I experience and enjoy when I'm playing tennis and golf, so that's what made this chapter fun to write. The legendary actress Katherine Hepburn once said, "If you obey all the rules, you miss all the fun." I have that quote inscribed on a needlepoint pillow in my office.

It's much easier living it up than living it down. Like Smith and Brown who were playing off in the club championship and are all tied walking over to the eighteenth hole. Smith knocks his ball into the rough to the left. He and Brown look for it for awhile, but when they can't find the ball, Brown goes back to the fairway, hits his ball onto the green and ostensibly wins the match. Suddenly, Smith yells, "I've got it! I found it!" So Smith hits his ball up on the green stonie for a gimme birdie 3. Brown's so flabbergasted that he two-putts for a 4 and loses. The question is, "What would you do if you're Brown—and have Smith's ball in your pocket?"

The "gotcha" story is another one of my favorite golf tales. Two golfers are getting ready to play. One is definitely a better golfer than the other, so he offers to give the poor player a ten-stroke handicap in the match. The poor player says, "No, I'd rather have two gotcha's than ten strokes." Having no idea what a "gotcha" is, he agrees, figuring two gotcha's couldn't change the outcome. As the better player starts his back swing, the poor player hits him very hard across his rear end with the handle of his driver. He completely misses the shot and wonders what's going on, when he hears the poor player say, "That's one gotcha!" From that moment on, every time the better player addresses the ball, the poor player stands behind him with his driver in his hand. It's obvious how the match turned out.

Having played as much golf as I have, I have heard more than my share of golf jokes on the course. These three are among my favorite one-liners. "I'm playing so badly that I lost two balls in the ball washer today." "I'm hitting the woods fine. I'm just having trouble getting out of them." And "I'm playing so badly I have already re-gripped my ball retriever twice this year."

Here's another for golfers: A fellow gets up on the first tee and takes out a new sleeve of balls with lakes to the left and lakes to the right. He knocks a new ball out into the lake to the left. Takes another new ball out and hits it in the lake to the right, then hits another new one into the lake on the left again. The fellow playing with him says, "Hey, why don't you use an old ball?" The first guy says, "I never have any."

∞

When you're in the business of golf, it's important to know all you can about as many courses as you can. I love to play at other people's courses because I learn from our competitors. And I consider golf books a real treat. For someone who learned golf from masters like Sam Snead, Ben Hogan, Byron Nelson, and Ralph Guldahl—all U.S. Open champions—I am sometimes chided that I ought to play better than I do. I agree. At my age, I don't play golf or tennis as well as I once did, but I still think I should be better because I know so much more about technique. Just like the fisherman and the whopper that got away, however, every golfer has a story to tell about his or her best round of golf. Mine is fun to talk about, and, despite my age, I remember it well. I actually shot my age when I was sixty-five. I had a hole in one, and two eagles in one round so I was six under par on three holes. I've never done that before, or since. The round was on the President's Course at Brookhaven, only about a 6,100-yard course, but it's still golf. It seems like the older I get, the better I *was* in both golf and tennis, in my own mind. But my goal remains to shoot my age again.

ENGRAVED INVITATIONS

We wouldn't commit to a city club unless we could recruit a Board of Governors, who were chairmen or presidents of companies for whom 80 percent of the people in the community either worked for, sold to, or borrowed from. That way, we had instant credibility, image, and clout. We recruited people like Henry Ford in Detroit, Lamar Hunt in Dallas, and former Sears & Roebuck Chairman Arthur Wood in Chicago. In smaller cities, the pattern was the same.

We were methodical about it. We'd have the bankers write invitation letters to their borrowers, and buyers like Ford Motors and Sears & Roebuck write to their suppliers. They'd write, "Would you like to join with us in our new club?" It was an invitation few could refuse.

11

Like Nobody's Business

The club business is run like nobody's business because it is nobody's business. Just about everything that's ever been written about me or ClubCorp includes that sentence, because it's something I've said repeatedly for many years. I say it a lot because it says a lot in a hurry. And, in a nutshell, it's the major management principle, when added to Robert's Rules of Order, that has been key to the success of ClubCorp. The "nobody's business" quote does explain my rationale for the business strategy and why the company became successful. We run our clubs like businesses. We run other people's clubs like businesses too.

Most clubs are run like nobody's business because they are nobody's business. They're managed by the members themselves who are amateurs when it comes to the club business. Members join country clubs to enjoy themselves, not to agonize over the club's business or be presented with a new set of problems to solve every time they show up. In most cases, the more successful, business-savvy people who are members don't volunteer to take part in the running of the club. They'd rather leave business behind when they go play. That puts the business of running the club in the hands of members who are less successful and experienced in business. These people have good intentions. They just don't have the expertise. They don't know what "par" is in the club business. They don't know how many people ought to be maintaining the golf course, or what the budget should be. They typically don't have comparable experience, and so they rely on lots of committees. Form a committee to study this. Form another one to analyze that. And guess what? Nothing ever gets done as well as it should.

Despite an ailing golf handicap, I often say I'd gladly play the five best golfers in the world if they all had to hold the club at the same time and decide how to swing it. It's like the old saying that a camel was really a horse designed by a committee of country club members. Another "ditty" I've used frequently is, "If you want discussion a-plenty, have a committee of twenty. If you want to get things done now and then, have a committee of ten. If you really want to get things done, have a committee of one." Or, "For God so loved the world he didn't send a committee to save it." In my book, club committees should look after the fun stuff, such as golf, tennis, and social activities, and ClubCorp should look after the business. We have Boards of Governors in all our clubs that basically serve as advisory boards, and we listen to them—real loud.

∾

To be a good entrepreneur, you have to know how to intelligently use what we call OPM, "Other People's Money," and more importantly than that, OPB, "Other People's Brains." As a good steward, you really do have to make maximum use of both, but the "other people" have to win, too, or they won't continue to work for you or do repeat business with you. Franklin Roosevelt once said, "I'm not the smartest fellow in the world, but I can sure pick smart colleagues." I have a whole legion of partners to prove that. And I still have an incredibly profound respect for the successful utilization of OPM and OPB.

When we started Brookhaven, I immediately enlisted all my friends in the project. I pushed all the chips out to the center of the table and rolled the dice. We rallied some folks together and shared the concept with them—three country clubs in one and being able to provide a better product for a better price. They all agreed to be a part of it. We created a Board of Governors composed of some of the leading people in Dallas at the time. Jack Dale, who had his own paper business, was the first club president at Brookhaven and even served as best man at our wedding. Clark Breeding was senior partner at Peat Marwick Mitchell, one of the world's largest accounting firms at the time. Dave Fox of Fox and Jacobs was the largest home developer in Dallas. They were all sensational people. I was their lawyer too, and we're still friends.

That was really an interesting time in my life because the concept worked. Collectively, we were able to enroll a lot of members in a hurry who paid us large enough initiation fees to be able to build the first phase of Brookhaven. The concept was valid, and because of that, we were able to pull it off.

ଓ

I fondly remember Chuck Bishop, our first membership sales director. His background was in car sales, and he needed every bit of that expertise when he started to sell memberships at Brookhaven. Chuck rolled up his sleeves, tucked the sole rendering of the club, several fact sheets, and membership application forms under his arm and came back with more than a thousand completed applications with checks attached. To his everlasting credit, Chuck put more than $1 million in sales in the bank before construction began. His sales pitch was simple. We were bringing a Cadillac to town for Chevrolet prices. We were going to have Cadillac facilities in golf, tennis, swimming, art, flowers, people, services, and programs—for less than one-half the cost of most eighteen-hole clubs. Our starting initiation fee at Brookhaven for an entire family was $280, compared to the Dallas Country Club's $10,000 initiation fee. Some people didn't think we could make a club work for so little money. Initial life memberships were $1,000. These life memberships were the best value anybody ever got in a club membership. Monthly dues were $12.80. Brookhaven was built on money from memberships, not fancy ways of financing like we have today. Obviously, we didn't start construction until we had sold enough memberships to guarantee completion of the club's first phase. If we didn't sell memberships, we couldn't meet our construction payments on the subsequent phases.

This dependency on memberships coined a familiar question for our executives. On a daily basis, I'd ask, "Partner, what's your CIF's for today?" That stood for "Cash In Fist." CIF's were our bread and butter while Brookhaven was under construction. We were also clever in marketing. One technique we used involved shills. Remember hatcheck girls? They use shills, too. They would put a two-bit piece, four bits or a dollar bill in a saucer to suggest to other people that they do the same. Bartenders do something similar by having big brandy snifters full of money in sight on the bar. We would put a stack of membership application forms with different color checks attached on the top of Chuck's desk. When someone came into the office and signed up, Chuck would just take his or her application and put it on top of the stack. We wanted to create a sense of urgency and momentum. No one wanted to be the only one buying an Edsel. We were trying to push something like a land sale syndrome.

You're there and you'd better buy it while you still can before we ran out of land or memberships to sell.

Actually, when it came to memberships, we really tried to steer clear of the term "sell." We didn't "sell" memberships. We "matriculated" members. We took applications for people to become members, and we wanted them to "enroll." We ran advertisements to that effect, and I would usually write them. The ads read, "Apply for membership today," not "Buy a membership today." We implied that if you wanted to be a member, you had to be approved.

As another sales technique, we also required three personal references, as well as two bank references, on each application. We did this for two reasons. First, we wanted them to feel like we were not just taking in anybody who could write a check. Secondly, we knew that the references would be good ones. Nobody's going to put somebody down as a reference who's going to say something bad about them. Then we'd call their references and say, "Bill Jones has given you as a reference to join Brookhaven," and they'd ask, "What's that?" This was also a way of telling everybody that so-and-so had joined and our getting bank references made the process seem more selective. We matriculated a heck of a lot of members through personal references. We'd also write them. Sometimes they wrote back or called to ask, "What's Brookhaven? Tell me about it." Or they'd go back to the person who'd given them as a reference and ask, "What's this new club that you just joined?" Everything we did in sales and marketing was set up to get bigger and be the best.

∾

It was quite a milestone when the swimming complex at Brookhaven Country Club opened in 1958. The first golf courses and other sports activities followed in 1959, but that's not to say we were spared some painful agonies along the way. One potential disaster really wasn't anybody's fault. I guess if somebody had released the pressure plug, it might not have happened. But that's a little like playing Monday-morning quarterback. Early on in our existence, about 1961, some of our people emptied the Olympic pool to clean it right before a torrential downpour. Then something terrible happened. The water went underneath the pool and pushed it up out of the ground about eleven inches on the northeast corner. How to fix that thing was a real problem! What we finally ended up doing was taking blowtorches and cutting off what was sticking up out of the ground, then leveled off the pool, re-tiled it and re-leveled the surrounding deck. The whole thing changed the depth from twelve feet to eleven feet on the northeast end of the pool. That one incident probably cost us about $75,000 to $100,000, which in itself wasn't that much. But it was significant, considering that expenditure wasn't in the budget, and it took away money that we had planned to spend elsewhere. The timing was traumatic, too, because it happened just before the swimming season. There were countless interruptions in schedules for swimming leagues and lessons and team sports. But we survived our own version of "El Nino" back then by having the adult and junior pools and using them more while we repaired the Olympic pool as quickly as possible.

∾

Another benchmark came when the doors to Brookhaven's main clubhouse swung open on Easter Sunday, 1960, some two years and nine months after our initial announcement of the club's organization. When it was built, Brookhaven was the world's largest private country club. That same distinction holds true today, as a testimony to what Henry Ford once said, "You can't build a reputation on what you are going to do." Its lush surroundings play host to a thriving country club with three eighteen-hole golf courses, forty-one tennis courts (sixteen of which are indoors), nine racquetball courts, five swimming pools, and an athletic club. There's even a nursery for the little ones in order to encourage members to come to the club as a family.

As I supervised Brookhaven's construction and its subsequent growing pains, I literally had a law vocation and a business avocation. I continued to practice law for the first seven years of ClubCorp's existence. I cut back my practice of law from eighty hours a week to sixty hours, and spent twenty hours a week nights, weekends and holidays, in a sense moonlighting, to start ClubCorp. I never considered myself a workaholic, even at eighty hours a week. To me, a workaholic is someone whose only thrust in life is work. In my case, I didn't want to cut the umbilical cord to a super law practice that obviously saved us a lot of money in legal fees and reduced the need to take out a significant salary from the company to support my family. My vocation was a good subsidy to my avocation.

This part-time status, though, forced me, and at the same time, enabled me, to get and keep better people. I had to become a lot more aware of the management art. I had to learn how to attract good people, properly compensate and motivate them, and maintain the proper interface with them. I think I was able to get and keep better people than I might have, had ClubCorp been a founder-dominated company. I had to depend on them, and they knew it. You've probably heard very few founders of a company say the main reason for their company's success is that they, as the founder, didn't have that much to do with it. In my case, it's true. From the very beginning, the more our people did and the less I did, the better we did. Our people enjoyed hearing me say this because it was both true and motivational at the same time.

∾

About a year before Brookhaven was completed, Chuck Bishop went west to matriculate members for us for a similar club in the Los Angeles, California, area. It had the same basic concepts that helped make Brookhaven so successful, except the numbers were a little different. It had only two eighteen-hole golf courses built around one clubhouse. Looking back, we were pretty clever in how we started promoting Braemar Country Club. Under California's securities law, all memberships in a new club had to be sold at the same price, which meant that we couldn't raise the price after every two hundred members or so as an incentive to joining early, or what I like to call an "anti-procrastinator." All of its promotional materials had to be approved by a $600-a-month administrator who worked for the state and had never belonged to a club. That set-up made promoting a new club practically impossible, but you could legally expand an existing club without going through this administrator and the attendant expense and delay.

So I said, "Why don't we just buy an existing club and expand it?" And we did. We bought the Deauville Beach Club in Santa Monica, which was built in the 1920s and had an indoor swimming pool and a beautiful beach on the Pacific Ocean. After the purchase, we called it the Deauville Golf and Beach Club. It was a huge building, something over 100,000 square feet, with the biggest indoor swimming pool in America at the time. Somebody could join and immediately become a member of and use the beach club while we were building the country club in the San Fernando Valley about fifteen miles away. We were able to buy the beach club for $50,000 down from Banker's Life. As I recall, the total price was $250,000 with $50,000 down and $50,000 each year for four years. It was less expensive than getting a securities permit and we could start immediately. The members could join today and swim today. Or play on the beach today while we were building the country club. After we opened the golf course, the members voted on whether we should keep the beach club or sell it and put the money into the golf courses. When they voted to sell it, we did and made money in the process.

When Braemar Country Club opened in 1961, the success came quickly. The developer of the surrounding residential community bought three hundred memberships in the club before the ink was dry on his deal—especially when we agreed to change the name from Deauville to Braemar (to match the subdivision's name) and sold him three hundred memberships at the same time. Talk about a win-win deal for both of us! With the opening of Braemar, our size as a company doubled in the blink of an eye. We now had two clubs. What's more, the members at Brookhaven enjoyed full privileges at Braemar, and vice versa. Privileges at Associate Clubs (outside a certain radius of members' home clubs) were founded on the principle that the clubs would be a haven of refuge and a home away from home for our members. I think part of the nobility I felt in starting ClubCorp was the reward of creating a facility for anyone who worked hard enough to afford such a refuge. But we couldn't go forward and get bigger as a company without a success or two. Brookhaven and Braemar were our deliverance. They were the proof in our pudding. We were creating a brand new market with our members' help, and everybody knew it. I hate to say it because today's peacock is tomorrow's crow, but I'm sure there were times that we looked like proud peacocks strutting around with our tail feathers called Brookhaven and Braemar.

I remember the years that followed as if they were part of a kaleidoscope: Many different things were happening at the same time. The company was going in diverse directions, but doing so with fortitude and forethought. The clubs prospered and the overall company grew at a phenomenal rate of 30 percent per year. For years, I displayed "30 PCT" on the license plate of my car like a proud papa. Just how fast ClubCorp grew is a difficult topic to embrace because our success inspired awe in all of us involved. There were times that I felt like I was watching "Jack

---

The Rule of 72

I'd like to share a convenient financial-planning technique that's called The Rule of 72. It's used to calculate the number of years that it will take your money to double on any level of compounding interest rate. All you do is divide the compounding interest rate into 72. For example, if you're receiving a compounding interest rate of 6 percent, it'll take twelve years for your money to double. If you're receiving a rate of 12 percent, your money will double in six years, or a rate of 10 percent, it'll double in 7.2 years.

The same rule applies on the compounding percentage growth of your net profits or gross revenues. If your net profits and/or gross revenues are compounding at 12 percent a year, it'll take six years for them to double. If a company is growing at 10 percent per year, it will double its revenue every 7.2 years. If it's growing at 20 percent per year, it will double every 3.6 years.

This rule applies whether you're dealing with five billion dollars or five dollars. It's a technique that has worked for ClubCorp over the last forty-one years ... and it can work for you.

---

and the Beanstalk" in living color. If I stood back and took a deep breath, I felt I could watch the beanstalk grow up and up and up into the clouds until I couldn't see the top anymore. From 1957 to 1965, we opened three clubs, one every year and nine months. From 1965 to 1970, we opened seven clubs, a new club every ten months. Then our beanstalk took off. In 1971, five new clubs came aboard to give us a total of fifteen. The year 1972 took the company to twenty clubs and 1973 added two. By the end of 1974, the total was thirty-six; 1975, forty-nine. When we purchased the Inverrary Country Club in Fort Lauderdale, Florida, in 1975, we hosted our first major PGA Tour tournament. Within the first six months of 1976, we already had six more new clubs for a total of fifty-six. We'd gone from one new club every three years to one a month in what seemed to me like overnight.

And we continue to grow internally and externally. Braemar became the impetus for what today we call the Associate Club system, which includes more than two hundred CCA and non-CCA clubs on five continents. The program gives reciprocal membership privileges to members at clubs outside a fifty-mile radius of their home club. In recent years, this concept has been expanded to encompass the "society" of clubs, perhaps one of the hottest innovations in membership trends in many years. Across the country now, societies affiliated with ClubCorp properties, and often other private clubs in selected metropolitan areas, are adding value and options to an individual member's benefits by providing reciprocal privileges within their home regions.

A private club represents a multiplicity of highly-specialized businesses, such as golf, tennis, merchandising, landscaping, fitness, entertainment, and food and beverage. When you consider the lifetime of training, experience, and full-time effort needed to successfully operate just one of these businesses, it's almost overwhelming to think of the energy needed to learn how to operate a club that contains them all. When we acquire a new property, we try to keep as many employee partners as we can. We want to start showing improvement as quickly as possible, and that's hard to do if we're bringing in a lot of people from the outside who don't know the members, the facilities, or the community. We keep as many as we can, and bring in people we call "coaches," regional vice presidents who try to help them in whatever area they need help. The football coach at Tennessee one time paid Bear Bryant at Alabama the ultimate compliment. He said, "He can take his players and beat you, or he can take your players and win." That's one of the things that we like to think we do best. We have good coaches.

Another advantage that we have over competitors is that

while many private clubs charge monthly minimums for food or assess members annually to cover losses, we don't. We cut costs immediately by making a club we purchase part of our bulk-buying operation. We use the same exact financial report at every club we own. That way, we're always aware where each club is, from week to week and year to year, and we compare it to the other two hundred-twenty-plus clubs in our network. If electricity payments at a club have increased over the same period the previous year, we know immediatley and we find out why. We have a weekly operations plan at every property, and we'll have an accountability meeting to see how we did at the end of the week. That keeps all of our people right on top of the numbers. And by keeping numerical scores in every department, we can't kid ourselves with adjectives. It's like players in a golf tournament. When they finish their round of golf, the only thing that determines how well they did is a number. Best number at the end of the tournament wins. It's that simple.

BORN TO SERVE OTHERS

One of my favorite sayings goes like this: "Attitude affects teamwork; teamwork affects members; members affect paychecks; paychecks affect attitude." We hire attitude over aptitude, which is determined by a battery of psychological tests and a formal screening process. We do this because we want people who really feel that it is noble to turn someone else on. One of our city club managers, who was particularly good at what he did, once said to me, "Bob, you were born to be an executive. I was born to be a maid." What he meant was that he was born to serve and service is a very noble thing. We push very hard for attitudes like his. We try to attract it, keep it, motivate it, and reward it. Just like givers foster other givers and takers spawn other takers, good people attract good people. Being able to recruit and retain good people is a compliment to the people we already have. I like to think of myself as a good motivator of people and an insightful recognizer of a job well done.

12

How I Grew Rich in Money Too

As we hired better and better people with terrific attitudes, our country club operations grew. In turn, this core growth allowed us to expand even more, taking us right up to where we are today—poised for a new millennium and looking ahead. Looking back, there were benefits even during tough times. Our troubles made us a better company. We became better listeners. And better listening meant better sales which meant more repeats and referrals. So let me back up a minute to show you how we got to here.

The decade of the 1960s took the company into consulting work for other people's clubs. This venture produced many good things—more cash, better knowledge, a bigger core of key people, a larger force of capable managers and staff support, even knowledge of more deals in more markets. Between 1959 and 1970, we were consultants for more than fifty clubs scattered from California to Massachusetts and New Jersey to Wyoming. You could practically call the roll of clubs in any given area of the country and we had a presence there. The impetus for this business explosion was a 1961 front-page story in the *Wall Street Journal* about private country clubs and their financial and management problems. The article portrayed us as a money-maker and touted our successes in an industry plagued with failures—and essentially opened up the vista of management consultation.

In 1970, we decided to forego the consulting business and concentrate on developing our own base of country clubs and city clubs. We changed our name from Country Clubs, Inc., to Club Corporation of America to reflect our wider range of activity. CCI didn't disappear; it just became managed by ClubCorp. The creation of ClubCorp also served as a vehicle for our employee partners to participate in the company through stock ownership plans. What then followed was a tremendous growth spurt. We expanded the city club concept by opening our first city/athletic club, the University Club of Houston. This club was developed in conjunction with a large, upscale Gerald Hines commercial and retail complex known as the Galleria. His complex featured an innovative indoor ice-skating rink. Our club was home to the first indoor climate-controlled tennis complex in the world. Our first city-athletic club combo also incorporated workout facilities, squash, tennis, and swimming with low-fat "Heart Healthy" cuisine, as well as fine dining.

൭

One of the beauties about city clubs has been our ability to tailor them to different markets. In Chicago, we started a club in the Prudential Building after a club, popular with chief executives and other top managers, moved to Standard Oil of Indiana's newer—and taller—building across the street. Since the local market for chief executives had already been captured, we designed a club strategy to attract upper, middle, and senior management. The Metropolitan Club in the Sears Tower remains one of our most exclusive by requiring prospects to produce three letters of recommendation from members.

We have been just as strategic about choosing our financial partners too. Developers of Class-A office buildings like to have city clubs in their buildings for many reasons. The primary reason is that city clubs help establish or position the building as a premier business location by attracting and retaining the best tenants at premium rental rates. Historically, we have protected our partners by not building a club until we have achieved a "trigger" by pre-selling enough memberships through the efforts of the Board of Governors and ourselves facilitating the process. If we did not achieve the trigger we would refund the membership deposits back to the members. By not starting construction until we knew the club was going to be economically viable it allowed us to ensure the success of the club and make it a valuable asset to our partners and the community. I have always liked to say we took all of the risk until there was no risk. City clubs are becoming popular in the emerging international markets too, such as the one we recently finished in Singapore. We raised $25 million in initiation fees before the club opened—to build a $15-million club. I'm pleased it's been such a good launching pad for our expansion in Asia...and the rest of the world.

∾

By 1980, ClubCorp had opened ninety-seven clubs and developed an enviable reputation for buying failing clubs in "fire sales" and then turning them around. We don't specialize in disaster deals anymore but buying and managing clubs that were in trouble did extend our reach across the nation. This strategy also opened the door to resort development in the mid-1980s, and since then, the company has established itself as a major resort operator. We purchased Pinehurst Resort & Country Club in

North Carolina from a consortium of eight banks. The venerable Pinehurst was losing $1 million a year before we acquired it in 1984. We thought we could take it to $2 million operating profit the first year. We actually took it to $4.5 million.

We decided to try our hand in public fee golf courses in 1986 with the acquisition of Silband Sports Corporation, adding 11 properties with that single purchase. Today, ClubCorp manages about forty public golf courses and is the nation's second-largest public golf course owner and operator. With golf's popularity at an all-time peak, courses are opening at a rate of more than one a week. For all of our management skills, golf is a catalyst for much of our success and an important competitive edge in the resort business. Hotel and motel management schools don't teach about the psyche of the golfer—something we have been learning about for more than forty years.

ClubCorp Realty, a real estate development arm originally formed in 1976 to develop residential communities around our country clubs, is active in land acquisition and development of large-scale, master-planned communities surrounding resorts and daily-fee golf properties.

❧

We had our share of problems to solve at ClubCorp in the 1980s, as well. One of the reasons that we were able to climb back up was our investment philosophy. We made sure that we never bet the farm or the cow. We would bet just the milk from the cow. We would only risk one year's income and were always good stewards of our members' funds. We never gambled with money that they had bet on us. It was very sad to see some of my friends going broke in the 1980s and early 1990s. Many people that I'd grown up with in business bit the dust. We didn't, but the recession was hard on me and it was an effort at times to see the bright

Footprints

To paraphrase what Longfellow once wrote, "*The lives of all great people remind us that we can make our lives sublime, and departing leave behind us footprints in the sands of time.*"

It's not too often in life that anyone is fortunate enough to be able to preserve and enhance golf institutions and communities like ClubCorp has. In 1993, we acquired $100 million worth of properties, including the two-hundred-year-old Homestead resort in Hot Springs, Virginia, set on 15,000 acres in the Allegheny Mountains. Started in 1766, ten years before the American Revolution, The Homestead is the country's oldest resort and now also offers superb golf. Thomas Jefferson designed the spa, which is still in use. George Washington even wrote a letter to his officer corps, suggesting they come to the hot springs at The Homestead to heal their war wounds. The Homestead has the oldest Number One golf tee in continuous use in America, which dates to 1891 and features a United States Golf Association plaque designation.

Pinehurst Resort and Country Club now is the largest golf resort in the world with eight eighteen-hole courses. Many refer to the property reverently as "The Golf Capital of the World." Its famous No. 2 course is the location of the next U.S. Open.

The Upper Cascades course at Homestead is typically ranked fourth in the country and Pinehurst No. 2 second among courses available to the public. These rankings by *Golf Digest* change slightly from time to time, but to have two of the top four is something that's fun.

Like Longfellow, we recognize the important stewardship role in acquiring these properties and enhancing them so that they'll become better and prosper forever. These noble acts of preservation have a sense of eternity that means more to me than accumulating earthly resources.

side. I had good friends with large companies lose everything. They bet everything they had on their company or on one or two deals and lost the farm. The recent drop in oil prices has reminded others besides me of the 1980s oil bust, I'm sure. But what a difference twelve years has made. The oil industry contributed 18 percent to the state's output and 5 percent to employment in the 1970s. Today, those figures have shrunk to about 7 percent of output and 2 percent of jobs. Other industries continue to burst onto the scene, more than making up any losses from oil. The high-technology industry has replaced oil and is now our state's leading export, surpassing energy in output and employment. The oil and gas industries combined, which include petrochemicals, petroleum refining and the manufacture of oil and gas equipment, have shriveled from 25.8 percent of the state's output in 1981 to 10.4 percent last year.

The same was true for ClubCorp. We weathered the economic storm and survived. Our decline in growth made us stronger and smarter. The real estate slump provided us with an opportunity to acquire properties that would not have otherwise been available. By 1989, we owned four resorts, including Pinehurst in North Carolina where the next U.S. Open will be held and the Barton Creek Country Club, an Austin, Texas resort begun by former Texas Governor and U.S. Treasury Secretary John Connally. Besides being clobbered by the savings and loan crisis, the value of many resorts was clipped by tighter tax restrictions on passive real estate investments. We saw purchase prices as low as 20 percent of what they had been, so we didn't waste much time snatching up those properties. We also rapidly became a force overseas after entering Taiwan in 1982. Within seven years, we had picked up eighteen city and country clubs in Asia, Australia, and Europe. As the 1990s draw to a close, we continue to expand internationally, such as our deal that makes ClubCorp the largest shareholder in European PGA Tour Courses Ltd., which owns top tournament venue courses in England, Sweden, Spain, and Portugal.

∾

ClubResorts, the unit spawned by our 1984 acquisition of Pinehurst, has made golf and conference resorts management and ownership one of the fastest-growing segments of our business. I believed the ClubCorp organization was better suited than commercial hotel firms to succeed in the golf resort business. Hotels are mainly in the linen-changing business and serve the eat-to-live mentality. We're in the business of looking after people who live to play golf and tennis and to eat and drink. We measure our success by the amount of repeat and referral business we get. We work hard to re-book resort guests before they ever leave, and remember their names when they return. We're more than 80 percent on repeats and referrals at Pinehurst. That's one of the reasons it's doing so much better now than when we bought it. We now own and operate, or manage, major resort properties in Quebec, Canada; California, Colorado, North Carolina, South Carolina, Texas, and Virginia. In fact, we've got the world-class properties when it comes to resorts. The world comes to Pinehurst Resort & Country Club, for example, which turned one hundred in 1995, and to the Homestead which was started in 1766.

∾

One of our most inspired efficiencies comes from the design of our golf courses. Over five million rounds of golf are played annually on ClubCorp courses. Over the years, we've found ways to reduce playing time without making our members feel like they're on a cattle call. The grass for the roughs is mowed short so errant golf balls don't take twenty minutes to find. Groves of trees are planted next to the tees so wild tee shots will stay in bounds. To keep the courses challenging for good players and still satisfying for less-skilled golfers, fairways are shaped like an hourglass. They are wide at about two-hundred yards from the tee so higher handicap players have plenty of room to land their shots, but narrow at two-hundred-fifty yards so good players will have to aim carefully to stay out of the rough. Since a beginners' shots usually will veer to the right, sand traps and water hazards are usually built to the left to help them keep up a good playing pace. These subtleties may seem too small to make a difference, but together they greatly reduce the average playing time, which means our courses are not only more pleasant to play but can also accommodate more golfers.

We've learned that enhancing and preserving nature is the best way to improve golf and increase land values. I should slip in a little joke by way of explanation: It seems a pastor was passing a parishioner tending to a flower garden. "Mrs. Smith, you and the Lord sure have done a great job with this garden," says the pastor. Mrs. Smith replies, "Yes, Pastor, I appreciate that, but you should have seen this mess when the Lord was taking care of it by Himself." When it comes to upgrading land values, we don't like to subtract from what nature's already given us. Sometimes we just add a little. We take great pride in what clubs and resorts can do to enhance the face of any community. We've planted hundreds of thousands of trees on the thirty-thousand-plus acres that we own in metropolitan areas around the country.

◦⌒

When the economy softened in the early 1980s, we pulled ourselves out of the doldrums by going back to "The Basics," a premise that we later formalized in writing as guiding principles for our business (listed in The Basics). The inculcation of "The Basics" into the hearts and souls of our employee partners is done with leaders who have the personal integrity to "walk the talk." One of the ways we share "The Basics" is through "line-up" discussions every morning at each of our operations worldwide and smaller segments at our home office. Every morning as the work day begins, an employee partner leads the discussion among a small group about one "Basic"—what it means and examples of how it works at various locations throughout the whole system. It's a team-building, spirit-building exercise, if you will, that gives "The Basics" a deeper meaning beyond words written on a laminated card.

Along with "The Basics," we also instituted "STAR Service" as a way to create value for all of our parnters. As the economy regained its strength, our efforts paid off. The company's earnings grew 20 percent in 1996 and 19 percent in 1997. Today, we're about $1 billion in revenue. Our growth rate in revenues and earnings provides a smorgasbord of pluses that we didn't have forty years ago. Knowledge. Expertise. A growing presence worldwide. Terrific employee partners. Greater purchasing and cross-marketing power. Scores of properties that we can point to with pride. And an incredible number of member partners who think we're great.

Our partnership culture and a belief in "Robert's Rules of Order" (and later The Basics and STAR Service) were keys to our success after we decided to decentralize club operations in 1985. We knew that we couldn't continue to meet aggressive growth goals—nor provide our member and employee partners with enough individual attention—with so much power concentrated at the top. We couldn't have the kind of large, monolithic structure with a pyramid shape that we had for years, and still know what was going on at the club level. We could better serve our members and our staff by pushing the decision-making down in the organization. The people who were dealing with the members every day had to be involved more in the management process.

∿

ClubCorp has come a long way in four decades. Pinehurst Resort & Country Club is the venue for the 1999 U.S. Open Championship, as I mentioned earlier. Firestone Country Club plays host to the NEC World Series of Golf every year; Indian Wells Country Club hosts one of the rounds of the Bob Hope Chrysler Classic every year; Mission Hills Country Club is the annual site of the Nabisco Dinah Shore, which is considered The Masters of the LPGA Tour. Other premier properties include The Homestead, Barton Creek, Daufuskie Island Club and Resort, Aspen Glenn, Mont-Sainte-Anne, and many others in the United States and abroad.

And I wear logos from them all on my shirts and hats. My wife teases me, suggesting I shouldn't wear my own logos as much as I do. But my comeback is an expression I've heard all my life: "It's a poor frog that doesn't praise his own pond."

Our purpose is to share the "Private Club Experience" with the world by creating "Pride In Belonging." Our Motto is: "The best serving the best." We have a passion for exceeding member expectations, and we keep it going with the three Steps Of Service: Warm Welcome, Magic Moments, and Fond Farewell. Our credo is to be a haven of refuge and a home away from home for the genuine care and comfort of our members. We strive to provide the highest levels of quality, personal service, and recognition with a commitment to continuous improvement. And we seek to establish traditions, build relationships, and create lasting value by listening, learning and serving our members' expectations, and having absolute integrity in everything we do.

These overall principles continue to give life to The Basics and STAR Service. Each employee partner carries a laminated card itemizing The Basics. STAR Service continues to represent the values, philosophies, and culture applied to every aspect of our business. The best part is that it offers daily opportunities to express our culture, and to earn recognition from members, guests, and fellow employee partners for their exemplary service.

STAR Service was conceived and implemented by my son, who's a star in my book. He took a leadership role in formulating the plan to take our company to a different level. What we're doing now is all about preserving the core, essence, values, and philosophies that make our business what it is—and at the same time, promote progress for the future. Kindred spirits. Shared values. Comradeship. A sense of belonging. A desire to please. We have goals. We have plans. My son and his leadership team have taken these important business concepts to new heights. Our employee partners have worked together, and, because of their efforts, we've reached our current plateau…and continue to ascend.

☙

My son has been a better company president and CEO than I ever was. He's using the same concept I always used very effectively: "The more the team does and the less I do, the better we do" and taken it to new heights. He is ClubCorp's biggest supporter of our partners being involved in the decision-making process. By making the decisions, these partners understand the reasons for a decision and have ownership of it. STAR Service is our future—to rally around, codify, revitalize, and enhance our corporate culture.

I had planned to retire, or at least begin to slow down, when I reached my sixty-fifth birthday. I'm seventy-two now and still haven't called it quits. I travel frequently from one club to another, have an incredible lecture circuit going, try to play golf every day and squeeze in time for tennis most weekends.

Would I do it all over again? You bet I would, especially when I think about where we started and how far we've come. We now have expert deal-makers combing the markets world-wide with our time-tested strategies. And there are still deals to be made, properties to be purchased and built, and goals to achieve. Some people call our clubs a haven of refuge. Others refer to them as a home away from home. I think of ClubCorp as the place where members are welcomed by name. The place where every need is anticipated, and every expectation more than fulfilled.

For more than four decades, our purpose has been to share the "Private Club Experience" with the world. Some might measure our success by the prestige of our premier properties, or by our size as the largest holding company for private clubs in the world. I measure our success in our passion to exceed our members' expectations. That passion has been my life. So much so, it's just too exciting to retire now. When someone asks me about the future, I feel like the mosquito flying over the wall of the nudist colony. It all looks so good, I don't know where to begin. I'd like to think, at ClubCorp, we're just getting started.

Epilogue

I heard a story once about Cecil B. DeMille when he was filming a movie called *The Flood*. They had dammed up a stream and were going to blow the dam to create the flood. Obviously, they didn't want to do that but one time, so he had three cameras set to film it and three of his best cameramen behind them to shoot the film. So they blow the dam, the waters come rushing out, and he yells out to the first cameraman, "George, did you get it?" George says, "No, the dynamite shook my camera cord loose." So he yells out to the second cameraman, "Bill, did you get it?" Bill says, "No, my camera cord came loose, too." Cecil thinks to himself, "I'm just sure ol' Sam got it because he's never let me down." So he yells out to his third cameraman, "Sam, did you get it?" Sam waves his arms and yells back, "Anytime you're ready, C.B."

Having now completed this project, my heart goes out to C.B. I hope I have captured in writing what C.B. was trying to get on film…a meaningful experience that's worth watching, or in my case, that's worth reading. In sharing some self-help tips, business how-tos, and personal insights that have influenced my life, I pray that I didn't bore you to death in the process. I'd hate to hear you say right now that your camera cord came loose. Or even worse, see you waving your arms and saying, "Anytime you're ready, Robert."

❧

This book has been fun to write. I hope it's been half as much fun to read.

Perhaps I've been able to shed a little light on the false importance of money. It's not how much or what you have in life that counts. Your ability to enjoy what you have—and forget about what you don't—makes the big difference. Money isn't the measure of any man or woman. Wealth beyond dollars and cents lives and breathes in the character of one's soul.

Now that I've reached the last of my life, I'm more attuned than ever before to Robert Browning's poem, "Rabbi Ben Ezra," written for his wife at a time in life when they were both aging. He wrote, "*Grow old along with me!/ The best is yet to be,/ The last of life, for which the first was made.*" Much of this book has revolved around the first of life. Robert's Rules of Order represent the guiding light that has illuminated my life. I'd like to think I've lived up to all of them reasonably well, because I've had one hell of a life. I don't apologize for enjoying life so much. I just wish everyone else would try it.

There are two guarantees in this lifetime of ours. First, we'll stay the color that we are born, and then one day, we'll die. Outside of that, we all have to work while we wait. Life is even better if we can figure out a way to have fun while we work. All it takes to be a big success is to work half a day—either the first twelve hours or the second twelve hours. Don't ever be afraid of hard work. It makes the rest of your life easy.

Our lives are a constant whirlwind of change. Those who adjust the best may be others like me who are in the last of life for which the first was made. If we've lived up to the principles outlined in this book about giving, living, loving, laughing, and having fun, then the last of life should be a ball. We've made our own heaven right here on Earth. We've seen a glimpse of the joy to come while we're still alive. And it feels good. We've watched our children grow up and now have their spouses and in-laws to add to the mix and enjoy. We have our grandchildren who are incredible blessings, and at least a handful of life-long friends whom we've obviously enjoyed for years, or we wouldn't still be friends. Hopefully, we don't have to worry about money or starting all over or climbing any more mountains. Our rapacious appetite to change the world has been diminished. I served as Chair of the Texas Board of Control, Purchasing and General Services Commission for two years and as Chair of the Texas Highway and Public Transportation Commission for two terms and am very proud of the progress made in both commissions while I served as their chair. Our suspicions are that we've done about all we're going to do, but we're happy. And we now have the privilege in the last of life to enjoy the fruits of our labor that consumed the first of life. In fact, we've probably lived longer because we've laughed more. We know now better than ever before what it means to be able to laugh at life…and at ourselves. And the more we do both, the happier and healthier and longer we'll live.

When I started ClubCorp, I was thirty-one and almost always the youngest person at every meeting. Today, I'm usually the oldest, so I've become a teller of a lot of geriatric jokes. I tell the younger executives, "You know…old age is a lot like a roll of toilet paper. It seems to go so much faster toward the end." Or, "The older I get, the better I was." There are even geriatric jokes about sex. "You'll be happy to know that us geriatrics still enjoy sex, particularly the one in the spring." And, "You'll also be happy to know that us geriatrics still make love nearly every night. Nearly on Thursday night. Nearly on Friday night. Nearly on Saturday night." Gets 'em every time.

∽

Monetary rewards aside, I have lived and am living the American Dream. I am doing what I love, loving what I do, and thanking God for both of those blessings. Happiness, after all, isn't something we get, but something we do. If what I have done makes me a "king" of clubs, then I hope that ClubCorp is such a good steward in all that it has done, is doing, and will do that all of our properties will be better, more beautiful, and more everlasting "footprints in the sands of time."

STAR SERVICE

ClubCorp Vision of Success

Purpose
To share the value of the "Private Club Experience" with the world by creating "Pride In Belonging."

Values
Personal Integrity and Character
The Member/Guest is King!
Plan Your Work and Work Your Plan
Win/Win Relationships
Continuous Growth

B-HAGs
(Big Hairy Audacious Goals)
Invited by a Partner
Waiting List to Belong
Know and Grow our Markets
Achieve Balanced
Scorecard Goals

Credo
We will be a haven of refuge and a home away from home for the genuine care and comfort of our Members and Guests.

We will establish traditions, build relationships and create lasting value by listening, learning and serving our Members' and Guests' expectations.

We will provide the highest level of quality, personalized service and recognition with a commitment to continuous improvement.

The Basics
The Basics are the values, behavior and best practices to help us achieve our Vision of Success.

VALUES

Our Values are what we believe, say and do

1. *Personal Integrity and Character*
Lead by example—be the first to Walk the Talk
Live by a Code of Conduct: trust, honesty, caring, respect, fairness, loyalty, diversity (people and thought)
Keep promises, exceed expectations and achieve results

2. *The Member/Guest is King!*
Vision: Meet and Exceed Member and Guest Expectations
Value = (Quality/Cost = Effective/Efficient)
Three Steps of Service
Listen, learn and serve

3. *Plan Your Work and Work Your Plan*
Begin with the end in mind, achieve desired results
Work smart, put first things first, do the right things right, plan to win
Prepare for future opportunities and challenges
Set aggressive goals (stretch)
Align personal, professional and business goals

4. *Win/Win Relationships*
Treat others fairly, balance the needs of all Partners
Live by the Employee Partner and Leadership Philosophies
Win their hearts and capture their minds
We're in the "repeat business" business

5. *Continuous Growth*
The best must be leaders in getting better
Share best practices and benchmark others
Be innovative, experiment and make suggestions (think big)
Grow revenues, manage expenses (spread management) and grow profits

P.R.I.D.E.

*We use P.R.I.D.E. to create Pride in Belonging for Members
and Guests, Employee Partners and Financial Partners.*

6. *Personalized Service*
Treat them all the same by treating each one differently
Know each person's interests and preferences
Anticipate needs—be proactive and not reactive

7. *Recognition and Acceptance*
Call everyone by name
Celebrate successes as a team and recognize individuals for their contributions
Acknowledge special occasions (birthdays, anniversaries, accomplishments)

8. *Involvement and Communication*
Active Boards, Committees and Task Forces
Capture our heritage and establish traditions
Actively listen, have open and honest dialogue
Involve Partners in decision-making

9. *Developing Relationships*
Live the Motto with all Partners
Grow friendships and relationships based on trust and mutual respect
Provide opportunities for networking and sharing of common interests
Be good stewards in your community

10. *Education and Growth*
Help others fulfill personal and professional goals
Provide access to educational opportunities and learning experiences (be a
    life long learner)
Share your knowledge and encourage others to do the same (be a teacher)
Fulfill your own potential

BEHAVIOR AND BEST PRACTICES

11. *Teamwork*
T.E.A.M. —Together Everyone Achieves More
Front and heart of the house "seamless service"
Create an environment of camaraderie
There is no "I" in team

12. *Fun/Humor*
Take our assignments seriously without taking ourselves too seriously
Have fun being in the "fun" business
Laughter is the shortest distance between two people

13. *Attitude*
Caring, genuine and from the heart with passion, enthusiasm and joy
Willing to serve others and have a servant's heart
Create a sense of urgency and a desire to win
Flexible, open-minded and willing to change
If you think you can or can't, you are right

14. *Aptitude*
Attitude plus aptitude determines altitude
Consistency and reliability in value
Learn and practice perfection for your role
Safety and protection of people and assets is every Partner's responsibility

15. *Atmosphere*
Uncompromising "Attention to Detail"
Make it white glove clean, take proper care and maintain the facilities
Know your role in emergencies and remedy hazards before they occur
Be environmentally responsible

16. *Service Recovery/Oops! Opportunities*
Treat mistakes as opportunities to learn
Make it more than right the second time
Only make original mistakes
Take the H.E.A.T. —Hear them, Empathize, Apologize, Take Action

17. *Personal Leadership*
Work within your circle of control and influence
The mirror test: "Am I living the values and achieving results?"
Be a role model and insist others be one too
Teach, coach and help others to succeed

18. *Personal Performance Management*
The three E's: Expectations/Equipping/Evaluation
Hire tough to manage easy; right person in the right job
Accept responsibility for your own performance
Have honest conversations
Develop a career plan to control your destiny

19. *Performance Value Systems*
Use and improve standards and systems
Feedback is the breakfast of champions
Proactively manage by the numbers
Measure our progress in achieving goals
Inspect what we expect

20. *Achieve Our Commitments and Goals*
Balance: Members and Guests, Employee Partners, Financial Partners
Help achieve commitment, not just compliance
Live the values and achieve results
Achieve the B-HAGs (Big Hairy Audacious Goals)
Create Pride in Belonging!

Clubs, Golf Courses, and Resorts

Club Corporation of America
Club Resorts, Inc.
The International Group of ClubCorp

The Clubline: 800-433-5079 · 972-999-7527 FAX

International callers: 972-888-7357 On the internet at www.clubline.com

ASSOCIATE CLUBS

ALABAMA

Summit Club	Birmingham	205-252-0088
Heritage Club	Huntsville	205-533-0350
Bienville Club	Mobile	334-433-4977
Capital City Club	Montgomery	334-834-8920

ARKANSAS

Diamante Country Club	Hot Springs Village	501-922-1114

ARIZONA

Gainey Ranch Country Club	Scottsdale	602-951-0022
Lakes Club	Sun City	602-974-6041
Metropolitan Club	Sun City	602-974-2219

CALIFORNIA

Cathedral Canyon Country Club	Cathedral City	760-328-6571
Center Club	Costa Mesa	714-662-3414
Coto de Caza Golf & Racquet Club	Coto de Caza	714-858-4100
Crow Canyon Country Club	Danville	925-735-5700
Diamond Bar Golf Course	Diamond Bar	909-861-8282
Eureka Municipal Golf Course	Eureka	707-443-4808
Paradise Valley Golf Course	Fairfield	707-426-1600
Rancho Solano Golf Course	Fairfield	707-429-4653
Airways Municipal Golf Course	Fresno	209-291-6254
Golden Era Golf Course	Gilman Hot Springs	909-654-0130
Tayman Park Golf Course	Healdsburg	707-433-4275
Indian Wells Country Club	Indian Wells	760-345-2561
City Club on Bunker Hill	Los Angeles	213-620-9662

Porter Valley Country Club	Northridge	818-360-1071
Desert Falls Country Club	Palm Desert	760-340-4771
Stoneridge Country Club	Poway	619-487-2138
Mission Hills Country Club	Rancho Mirage	760-324-9400
Canyon Crest Country Club	Riverside	909-274-7900
Teal Bend Golf Club	Sacramento	916-922-5209
University Club Atop Symphony Towers	San Diego	619-234-5200
The City Club of San Francisco	San Francisco	415-362-2480
San Francisco Tennis Club	San Francisco	415-777-9000
Capital Club Athletics	San Jose	408-292-1141
Silicon Valley Capital Club	San Jose	408-971-9300
Braemar Country Club	Tarzana	818-345-6520
Spring Valley Lake Country Club	Victorville	760-245-5356
Shadowridge Country Club	Vista	760-727-7700

COLORADO
Aspen Glen Club	Carbondale	970-963-4536
Metropolitan Club	Greenwood Village	303-694-7344
Fox Acres Country Club	Red Feather Lakes	970-881-2191

CONNECTICUT
| Hartford Club | Hartford | 860-522-1271 |
| Landmark Club | Stamford | 203-348-7381 |

WASHINGTON, D.C.
City Club of Washington, D.C.	Washington, DC	202-347-0818
Club at Franklin Square	Washington, DC	202-408-1300
George Washington University Club	Washington, DC	202-887-5030

DELAWARE
| Ed "Porky" Oliver Golf Course | Wilmington | 302-571-9041 |

FLORIDA
Countryside Country Club	Clearwater	727-796-2153
Halifax Club	Daytona Beach	904-252-3666
DeBary Country Club	DeBary	407-668-1705
Tower Club	Fort Lauderdale	954-764-8550
Haile Plantation Golf & Country Club	Gainesville	352-335-0055
Heritage Club	Gainesville	352-375-0578
Queen's Harbour Country Club	Jacksonville	904-220-2118
University Club of Jacksonville	Jacksonville	904-396-1687
Inverrary Country Club	Lauderhill	954-733-7550
Bankers Club	Miami	305-374-1448
Sabal Trace Golf & Country Club	North Port	941-426-4883
Country Club at Silver Springs	Ocala Shores	352-687-2828

Orange Park Country Club	Orange Park	904-276-7660
Citrus Club	Orlando	407-843-1080
Monarch Country Club	Palm City	561-286-8447
University Center Club	Tallahassee	850-644-8528
Centre Club	Tampa	813-286-4040
Hunter's Green Country Club	Tampa	813-973-1000
Tampa Club	Tampa	813-229-6028
Tampa Palms Golf & Country Club	Tampa	813-972-1991
La Cita Country Club	Titusville	407-383-2582
Governors Club	West Palm Beach	561-832-7577

GEORGIA

Buckhead Club	Atlanta	404-262-2262
One Ninety One	Atlanta	404-222-0191
Ravinia Club	Atlanta	770-392-7300
Northwood Country Club	Lawrenceville	770-923-2909
River North Country Club	Macon	912-746-2411
First City Club	Savannah	912-238-4548

HAWAII

| Plaza Club | Honolulu | 808-521-8905 |

IOWA

| Glen Oaks Country Club | West Des Moines | 515-221-9000 |

ILLINOIS

The 410 Club & Conference Center	Chicago	312-944-7600
Chicago Mercantile Exchange Club	Chicago	312-930-3050
Metropolitan Club	Chicago	312-876-3200
Monroe Club	Chicago	312-977-1350
Plaza Club	Chicago	312-861-3300
Meadow Club	Rolling Meadows	847-640-3200

INDIANA

Petroleum Club	Evansville	812-423-4422
Knollwood Country Club	Granger	219-277-1541
Skyline Club	Indianapolis	317-263-5000

KANSAS

| Crestview Country Club | Wichita | 316-733-1344 |
| Willowbend Golf Club | Wichita | 316-636-5555 |

KENTUCKY

| Lafayette Club | Lexington | 606-253-3406 |
| The Jefferson Club | Louisville | 502-584-1177 |

LOUISIANA

Camelot Club	Baton Rouge	504-387-0931
Belle Terre Country Club	LaPlace	504-652-5000
City Energy Club	New Orleans	504-524-3203
Southern Trace Country Club	Shreveport	318-798-8300
University Club of Caddo Parish	Shreveport	318-221-4330

MASSACHUSETTS

Boston College Club	Boston	617-946-2828
Ipswich Country Club	Ipswich	978-356-4822

MICHIGAN

Oak Pointe Country Club	Brighton	810-229-4554
Fairlane Club	Dearborn	313-336-4400
Renaissance Club	Detroit	313-259-4700
Skyline Club	Southfield	248-350-9898

MISSOURI

Media Club	St. Louis	314-241-8480

MISSISSIPPI

University Club of Jackson	Jackson	601-969-4011

NORTH CAROLINA

Carolina Club	Chapel Hill	919-962-1101
Providence Country Club	Charlotte	704-846-8475
Raintree Country Club	Charlotte	704-542-0800
Tower Athletic Center	Charlotte	704-333-1159
Tower Club	Charlotte	704-371-6460
Treyburn Country Club	Durham	919-620-0184
Capital City Club	Raleigh	919-832-5526
Piedmont Club	Winston-Salem	336-724-7077

NEVADA

Canyon Gate Country Club	Las Vegas	702-363-0303

NEW YORK

Athletic & Swim Club	New York	212-265-3490

OHIO

Akron City Club	Akron	330-376-5117
Firestone Country Club	Akron	330-644-8441
Cooks Creek Golf Course	Ashville	905-983-3636
Shoreby Club	Bratenahl	216-851-2587

Bankers Club	Cincinnati	513-651-3660
The Club	Cleveland	216-241-1272
Capital Club	Columbus	614-228-0225
Dayton Racquet Club	Dayton	937-224-4381
Quail Hollow Country Club	Painesville	440-350-3563
Silver Lake Country Club	Silver Lake	330-688-6066
Beckett Ridge Country Club	West Chester	513-874-2710

OKLAHOMA

Indian Springs Country Club	Broken Arrow	918-455-7431
The Greens Country Club	Oklahoma City	405-751-6266

PENNSYLVANIA

Treesdale Golf and Country Club	Gibsonia	724-625-2220
Middletown Country Club	Langhorne	215-757-6953
Cobbs Creek Municipal Golf Course	Philadelphia	215-877-8707
F.D. Roosevelt Municipal Golf Course	Philadelphia	215-462-8997
John F. Byrne Municipal Golf Course	Philadelphia	215-632-8666
Juniata Municipal Golf Course	Philadelphia	215-743-4086
Pyramid Club	Philadelphia	215-567-6510
U. S. Golf Sports Center	Philadelphia	215-879-3536
Walnut Lane Municipal Golf Course	Philadelphia	215-482-3370
Rivers Club	Pittsburgh	412-391-5227

SOUTH CAROLINA

Woodside Plantation Country Club	Aiken	803-649-3383
Harbour Club	Charleston	843-723-9680
Capital City Club	Columbia	803-256-2000
Commerce Club	Greenville	864-232-5600
Country Club of Hilton Head	Hilton Head Island	843-681-2582
Golden Bear Club at Indigo Run	Hilton Head Island	843-689-2200
Golf Club at Indigo Run	Hilton Head Island	843-689-5666
Snee Farm Country Club	Mt. Pleasant	843-884-8571
Pebble Creek Country Club	Taylors	864-244-8872

TENNESSEE

Walden Club	Chattanooga	423-756-6686
Club Le Conte	Knoxville	423-523-0405
Three Ridges Golf Course	Knoxville	423-687-4797
Crescent Club	Memphis	901-684-1010
Nashville City Club	Nashville	615-244-3693

TEXAS

Shady Valley Golf Club	Arlington	817-275-3092
Lost Creek Country Club	Austin	512-892-1205

Metropolitan Club	Austin	512-477-4447
Oakmont Country Club	Corinth	940-321-5599
Padre Isles Country Club	Corpus Christi	512-949-8056
Brookhaven Country Club	Dallas	972-243-6151
Brookhaven Heart Healthy Fitness Center	Dallas	972-243-2919
CityPlace	Dallas	214-828-7050
Tower Club	Dallas	214-220-0403
University Club of Dallas	Dallas	972-239-0050
Fair Oaks Ranch Golf & Country Club	Fair Oaks Ranch	830-981-9600
Fossil Creek Golf Club	Fort Worth	817-847-1900
Plantation Golf Club	Frisco	972-335-4653
Stonebriar Country Club	Frisco	972-625-5050
Bay Oaks Country Club	Houston	281-488-7888
Clear Creek Golf Club	Houston	713-738-8000
Clear Lake Golf Club	Houston	281-488-0250
Greenspoint Club	Houston	281-875-0191
Hearthstone Country Club	Houston	281-463-2201
Houston Center Club	Houston	713-654-0877
Houston City Club	Houston	713-840-9001
Houston Metropolitan Racquet Club	Houston	713-652-0700
Plaza Club	Houston	713-225-3257
University Club of Houston	Houston	713-621-4811
WestLake Club	Houston	281-556-5100
Westwood Country Club	Houston	713-774-2521
Atascocita Country Club	Humble	281-852-8111
Hackberry Creek Country Club	Irving	972-869-2631
La Cima Club	Irving	972-869-2266
Las Colinas Country Club	Irving	972-541-1141
Club at Falcon Point	Katy	281-392-7888
Deerwood Club at Kingwood Country Club	Kingwood	281-360-1060
Kingwood Country Club	Kingwood	281-358-2171
Kingwood Cove Golf Club	Kingwood	281-358-1155
Walnut Creek Country Club	Mansfield	817-473-6111
Tower Club	McAllen	956-686-2311
Club at Cimarron	Mission	956-581-7401
Quail Valley Country Club	Missouri City	281-437-7431
April Sound Country Club	Montgomery	409-588-1101
Club at Mission Dorado	Odessa	915-563-0980
Gleneagles Country Club	Plano	972-867-6666
Canyon Creek Country Club	Richardson	972-231-1466
Forest Creek Golf Club	Round Rock	512-388-2874
Northern Hills Country Club	San Antonio	210-655-4148
Plaza Club	San Antonio	210-227-4191
Timarron Country Club	Southlake	817-481-7529
Willow Creek Golf Club	Spring	281-376-1501

King of Clubs

Wildflower Country Club	Temple	254-771-1177
Brazos Club	Waco	254-776-5380
University Club of Wichita Falls	Wichita Falls	940-696-1968

Virginia

Greenbrier Country Club	Chesapeake	757-547-7375
River Creek Club	Leesburg	703-779-2022
Town Point Club	Norfolk	757-625-6606
Capital Club	Richmond	804-788-1400
Stonehenge Golf and Country Club	Richmond	804-378-7841
The Tower Club	Tysons Corner	703-761-4250

Washington

Columbia Tower Club	Seattle	206-622-2010

Wisconsin

Le Club	Milwaukee	414-352-4900

RESORTS

Pinehurst Resort & Country Club	Village of Pinehurst, NC	910-295-6811
Daufuskie Island Club & Resort	Hilton Head Island, SC	843-842-2000
Barton Creek	Austin, TX	512-329-4000
Homestead	Hot Springs, VA	800-838-1766
Mont-Sainte-Anne	Beaupre, Quebec, Canada	418-827-4561

INTERNATIONAL CLUBS

Capital Club	Beijing, China	011-86-10 6466-9098
Guayaquil City Club	Guayaquil, Ecuador	011-5934-690-510
Drift Club	Surrey, England	011-441-483-284641
POK-TA-POK, Club de Golf Cancun	Cancun, Quintana Roo, Mexico	011-52-98-831-230
Marina Vallarta Club de Golf	Puerto Vallarta, Jalisco, Mexico	011-52-322-10073
The Orchard Golf & Country Club	Dasmarinas, Cavite, Philippines	011-632-843-8344

City Club	Panama City, Rep. de Panama	011-507-210-1366
American Club	Singapore, Singapore	011-65 737-3411
Tower Club	Singapore, Singapore	011-65-737-3388
Mount Edgecombe Country Club	Durban, South Africa	011-2731-595-330
Silver Lakes Country Club	Pretoria, South Africa	011-2712-8090091

Vision
We have a Passion for Exceeding
Member
and Guest Expectations

Three Steps of Service
Warm Welcome,
Magic Moments,
Fond Farewell

Motto
The Best Serving The Best